Essays on
Alabama Literature

William T. Going

Essays on Alabama Literature

Studies in the Humanities No. 4

Literature

The University of Alabama Press

University, Alabama

Contents

ACKNOWLEDGMENTS

I gratefully acknowledge permission to use material in an earlier form from *The Georgia Review* for "Samuel Minturn Peck, Late Laureate of Alabama: *A Fin de Siècle* Study" (Summer, 1954) and "Philip Henry Gosse on the Old Southwest Frontier" (Spring, 1967). I also acknowledge permission from *The Alabama Review* to use material in several other essays that appeared in an earlier form in that journal. I gratefully acknowledge permission from the Estate of William E. Campbell (William March) and The Merchants National Bank of Mobile, especially its assistant trust officer, Lilian Jackson, to quote from the fiction and the papers of William March. To the University of Alabama Library I am grateful for permission to examine the papers of Samuel Minturn Peck before they were catalogued, and to its late librarian, Alice Wyman, for permission to quote from this material. To Mary Lee Leach Harwood, Peck's grandniece, and her husband Judge Robert B. Harwood I am grateful for advice and the same permission.

For personal help in answering questions about the lives of Zelda Sayre Fitzgerald and Sara Haardt Mencken I am especially indebted to Sara Mayfield and the late Andrew Turnbull. Acknowledgment to others for first-hand information is made in a special note at the end of the seventh essay. I also thank Selma Wolfman, secretary to Lillian Hellman, for information and advice.

For brief quotations for critical analysis from texts and from other critical studies about the Alabama authors considered here acknowledgment is implied within the body of the essays themselves.

I am indebted to Southern Illinois University at Edwardsville for research grants-in-aid and for a two-quarter sabbatical that made parts of this research possible. And to my wife, Margaret Moorer Going, I am grateful for help in preparing the various stages of this manuscript.

Edwardsville, Illinois   W. T. G.
June, 1974

Essays on
Alabama Literature

Introduction

PERHAPS the most distinguished Southern literature between World Wars I and II was that written by Mississippians. William Alexander Percy, Stark Young, William Faulkner, Hodding Carter, and Eudora Welty achieved, in varying degrees, popular acclaim and critical approval. More recent critical attention, however, is being turned toward the Southeastern seaboard with the work of William Styron, Reynolds Price, Flannery O'Connor, Carson McCullers, and James Dickey—Erskine Caldwell and Conrad Aiken having lived in and written about the region a generation earlier. In the 1920's and early 1930's the most lively Southern center of critical analysis and creative thought was the Nashville group: Allen Tate, John Crowe Ransom, Robert Penn Warren, Donald Davidson. Over a century ago William Gilmore Simms, Henry Timrod, and Paul Hamilton Hayne made Charleston the literary capital of the South.

Alabama, however, has been by-passed by those currents of environmental and intellectual stimulation that produce literary genius or those lesser writers seriously concerned with re-creating its region. In the *Literary History of the United States* (by Spiller, Thorp, Johnson, Canby, *et al.*) and in the bibliographical supplement (by Ludwig) Alabama is the only Southern state that has no separate entry in the bibliographical sections labeled "Regionalism" and "Movements"—and this in a region of which the editors comment: "No section of the country has been more conscious of its regionalism than the South." Alabama is bracketed with Tennessee, presumably because T.S. Stribling's trilogy—*The Forge, The Store,* and *Unfinished Cathedral*—deals with life in northwestern Alabama. Whether or not this judgment is a sound one, it is true that many of the best known names in Alabama letters remained only short periods of time in the state and often did not write about the local scene. In 1854, less than a year after the publication of *The Flush Times of Alabama and Mississippi,* Joseph G. Baldwin left the state to practice law in California. Immediately after the Civil War Sidney Lanier spent a much briefer time in South Alabama, where he wrote most of his war novel *Tiger-Lillies.* Father Abram J. Ryan's stay in Mobile was also a brief one, beginning in 1870; and Mary Johnston lived in Birmingham with her railroad-building father only from 1886 to 1902 when she was not away at school or spending months in New York. Most of her romance of Colonial Virginia, *To Have and To Hold,* she wrote in Birmingham, but with its publication she returned, after the death of her mother, to her native Virginia. And for only three years in the 1920's Carl Carmer taught at the University of Alabama and collected material for *Stars Fell on Alabama.*

At least two factors have militated against the creation of literature and literary criticism in Alabama. There has never been a major literary figure who has either lived in or consistently written about the state. There has been no Edgar Allan Poe, no William Gilmore Simms, no William Faulkner to serve as a bench mark or guiding star. And, second, there have been few influential literary groups with a publication to challenge and inspire local writers. The Charleston circle and their *Russell's Magazine* and *Southern Quarterly Review,* the Richmond *Literary Messenger* and later *Reviewer,* the

Nashville group and *The Fugitive,* as well as such eclectic journals as the *Sewanee Review, South Atlantic Quarterly, Virginia Quarterly Review, Southern Review,* and *Georgia Review* have no Alabama counterparts of any duration. The *Alabama Review,* founded in 1947, has published occasional essays on literature, but its primary interest has been the history of the state, since it is the organ of the Alabama Historical Association. The nearest approach to genial groups that have inspired one another has been the circle of young graduates of the first classes at the University of Alabama. A.B. Meek, who allied with young newspaper men in Tuscaloosa, like William Russell Smith, and with members of the University faculty, like F.A.P. Barnard, managed to perpetuate the *Southron* in Tuscaloosa for a few months in 1839. A second group in Birmingham in the 1920's, known as the Loafers, were sparked chiefly by Octavus Roy Cohen, Jack Bethea, and Edgar Valentine Smith. Their interest was primarily in fiction, and, aside from their novels, they published chiefly in national magazines like the *Saturday Evening Post* and *Harper's.* A third group of unique accomplishment has been the creative writing class of Hudson Strode at the University of Alabama from the late 1930's to the 1960's. In addition to the short story anthology, *Spring Harvest* (1944), the group has used national magazines for their short fiction; and many of the major publishing houses of the 1940's and 1950's, like Knopf, Rinehart, and Harcourt Brace, have issued first novels from young men like Robert Bowen, Borden Deal, and Robert Gibbons.

Aside from college literary magazines—like that sponsored at Howard College by A.H. Mason as well as his anthologies of young Alabama poets issued by the Studio Bookshop in Birmingham in the late 1920's—a lack of suitable local journals has disturbed Alabama writers for well over a century. In January, 1839, the "Introductory Salutatory" of the *Southron,* reminding its readers of the *Literary Messenger* at Richmond and the *Literary Journal* at Charleston, urged support and contributions about the "character and adventures of the pioneers and earliest emigrants to the South-Western States . . . . Of these fearless and hardy progenitors of the present population of the South-West, no memorials have been preserved." Suitable contributions followed: "Christmas in the Country—A Glimpse of Rural Life in Alabama" by William Russell Smith, "An Evening in Athens" by Henry W. Hilliard, "Sketches of the History of Alabama" by A.B. Meek, "A Legend of the Silver Wave" by Mrs. Caroline Lee Hentz, "Pettiboneville, Poetry and Posterity; or Passages in the Experiences of Jeremy Jumper" by Charles Augustus Conway [F.A.P. Barnard], a poem "To Miss . . . . . [Amelia Gayle (Gorgas)]" by F. [Francis] S. [Scott] Key (written in reply to a poem the little daughter of Governor Gayle had written for her distinguished visitor), and a review of William Gilmore Simms' *Richard Hurdis; or the Avenger of Blood,* "A Tale of Alabama." The literary contributions were forthcoming, but the sustaining cash and the subscribers were not.

Rhoda Ellison in *Early Alabama Publications* reports that no Alabama literary weekly or monthly lasted longer than five years, many only a few issues. Even the longest-lived, the Mobile *Southern Parlor Magazine,* founded in 1851, had to transfer its operations to Memphis in 1856 in order to prevent financial catastrophe. Augusta Evans Wilson of Mobile allows her literary heroine of *Beulah* (1859) to complain to a Southern editor:

> I happen to know that northern magazines are not composed of gratuitous contributions . . . . With the same subscription price, you cannot pay for your articles. It is no marvel then, under such circumstances, we have no southern literature.

Newspaper publication was equally unsatisfactory and far more ephemeral. Johnson Jones Hooper published his first humorous sketches in his *East Alabamian* at Lafayette and later in the New York *Spirit of the Times.* But if they had not been reprinted in book form as *Some Adventures of Captain Simon Suggs,* many would not now exist since there is no known complete file of these newspapers. Joseph G. Baldwin, on the other hand, first published his tales not in the newspapers of west Alabama where he lived at the time but in the *Southern Literary Messenger.*

In the 1890's Samuel Minturn Peck was still distressed by a lack of suitable vehicles for publishing his poems and stories. He resorted to the Boston *Evening Transcript* because the paper offered a dignified format for poetry, had a reasonably large circulation, and furnished him with unlimited offprints on slick paper; for his stories he used national publications. But in all his interviews in later years he regularly emphasized the fact that aside from newspaper publication the Alabama writer was without a local organ for his essays, poems, stories, and reviews.

About this same time John Trotwood Moore, who grew up in Alabama but later settled in Tennessee, was lamenting that so few writers seemed to realize the potential of raw literary material in the state. In "Alabama a Literary Field," quoted from an unidentified newspaper article of Moore's in Claude B. Green's *John Trotwood Moore: Tennessee Man of Letters,* the author of *Songs and Stories from Tennessee* states:

> There are few more inviting fields for literary work than Alabama. In historic setting it is rich indeed; and the local background is unique and most inviting. It has also the rarity of being new, in the sense that it has never been worked to the extent . . . of Georgia or Tennessee. For lack of the hands to do it, both of these states have far outstrip Alabama . . . .

And so it has gone: the lack of good writers and the lack of local publications to encourage good writing—these two factors have circularly repeated themselves.

It is not surprising, then, that the most familiar names associated for any length of time with Alabama letters before World War I were A.B. Meek, Caroline Lee Hentz, Augusta Evans Wilson, and Samuel Minturn Peck. All of these writers achieved a kind of "popular," if not critical, acclaim despite the literary climate of the region and the lack of local journals. The poetry and prose of Professor Meek had a local reputation because of its Byronic style and its treatment of Alabama legends (a matter which Welbourn Kelly has revived in his novel, *Alabama Empire*[1957]). At least a part of Meek's local fame grew out of the reprinting of his poems and stories in state histories and local school readers. Mrs. Hentz's novels of domestic sentimentalism sold over the 100,000 mark, and Mrs. Wilson achieved even greater national popularity with her novels like *St. Elmo,* which, according to its present publisher, has "over 1,000,000 copies in print." And the strange career of Samuel Minturn Peck is the subject of an essay in this volume.

Neither congenial literary friends, mentors, nor available journals will necessarily create whatever alchemy it is that encourages composition. Writing is essentially a lonely business: a process of understanding, withdrawing, and communicating. The right mediums of communication help, but they do not of themselves create writers.

The essays in this volume, which are designed to shed light on the Alabama literary scene, are not intended as a history of the literature of the state—if indeed there can be such a thing. In a country like ours where communication is nationwide and people are increasingly mobile, regional literary critiques and bibliographies are inclined to concern themselves with third-rate writers and with false distinctions about "native" authors, leaving the better men of letters to sink or swim in the tide of national and international criticism. Yet regional literary evaluation has its place, since setting and region often play a significant role in all forms of imaginative literature. What kinds of writers a state has produced or what fictional uses have been made of its background and environment speak clearly about the level of a state's culture.

This present group of essays is confined to a few writers or to a genre, and each essay treats its subject in some detail. The writers selected are those who have achieved a reputation of consequence but who have been neglected in the growing tendency of critical attention toward so-called "major" figures. No attempt has been made to define an Alabama author or to delimit Alabama literature; the aim has been wherever possible to relate whatever an author has written about the state to the larger literary scene to which he himself belongs and for which he writes.

In addition to Samuel Minturn Peck, I have discussed certain aspects of the Pulitzer novels of T.S. Stribling, Harper Lee, and Shirley Ann Grau as well as the novels and short stories of William March. Little serious criticism has been written about any of these authors, and in the cases of Peck and March I have had access to their papers, which unfortunately were not carefully preserved. Both men were wealthy bachelors who cared little for "keeping things"; neither posted a diary nor was a voluminous letter writer. Because March is by all odds the best and most voluminous craftsman of fiction about Alabama, I have devoted two essays to his work. His six novels and seventy-odd short stories are a vast repository of the times and temper of post Civil War Alabama. His Pearl County and its county seat of Reedyville are to Alabama what Faulkner's Yoknapatawpha and Jefferson are to Mississippi.

In the essay on Zelda Fitzgerald and Sara Mencken I have relied on the abundance of material about their husbands, as indicated in the bibliographical note appended to that essay, as well as on some first-hand accounts. Because these two Alabamians were interesting writers and personalities in their own rights, I have attempted to separate their lives and works from those of their more famous husbands.

Since there has been little written about the Alabama short story and no published anthology, the essay in this collection is a pioneering attempt. In the discussion I have tried to indicate some notion of the variety of short fiction written about the state during both the nineteenth and twentieth centuries.

Paul T. Nolan in "Alabama Drama, 1870-1916: a Checklist," in the *Alabama Review* of January, 1965, finds that only 55 residents of the state had copyrighted 71 dramas, that a considerable number of these appear to be dramatizations of stories and novels, and that only a few of the 71 were published. Since there has been so little drama written by Alabamians or even about Alabama, it seems wise to single out two distinguished dramatists who have written about life and people of the state, Augustus Thomas and Lillian Hellman.

One of the most accurate observers of the early years of Alabama was the English scientist Philip Henry Gosse, friend and antagonist of Darwin. His *Letters from Alabama* and his autobiographical essays, "arranged in [such] strict order" that they formed the basic document for his more famous son Edmund's *The Life of Philip Henry Gosse,* deserve to be better known. His Alabama sojourn I have made the subject of the last essay in this volume.

These essays, then, along with such studies as Rhoda C. Ellison's *Early Alabama Publications: A Study in Literary Interests* (1947), William P. Fidler's *Augusta Evans Wilson, 1839-1909: A Biography* (1951), and Stanley Hoole's *Alias Simon Suggs: The Life and Times of Johnson Jones Hooper* (1952), should begin to supplement and account for the Alabama literary scene. Though not intended as a literary history of the state, these essays because of a similarity of planning and style will form, I hope, representative perspectives on the fiction, poetry, drama, essay and letters about Alabama that have been infrequently examined.

1

Store and Mockingbird: Two Pulitzer Novels about Alabama

IN 1933 and 1961, over a quarter of a century apart, T.S. Stribling's *The Store* and Harper Lee's *To Kill a Mockingbird* received one of the Pulitzer awards granted annually for distinguished fiction dealing preferably with the American scene. Placed side by side they comment revealingly not only on life in two of the state's small towns fifty years and three hundred miles apart but also on the changing techniques of Southern fiction.

Maycomb of 1932-1935, the county seat of Maycomb County, is the locale of *Mockingbird*. This fictional town is "some twenty miles east of Finch's Landing . . . on the banks of the Alabama River" in the southwestern part of the state (Miss Lee somewhat obscures, intentionally or un-intentionally, its exact location by mentioning a Saint Stephens river—"the Saint Stephens"—and implying that old Saint Stephens, the territorial capital of Alabama, was located on the Alabama River, when it actually stood on the Tombigbee). Monroeville, county seat of Monroe County and birthplace of Miss Lee, who is the same age as her heroine, Jean Louise Finch, is the model for Maycomb. The chief locale of *The Store* is Florence of 1884-1885 in the north-western part of the state with a "long spindling bridge across [the] Tennessee" linking it with the rest of the state to the south.

The hub and center of both towns is the courthouse. In Maycomb the edifice, surrounded by live oaks, "sagged in the square"; it was of early Victorian design with its south portico supported by Greek revival columns left over from "the original courthouse that burned in 1856." It is the setting for the climactic scene of Atticus Finch's defense of Tom Robinson, a Negro accused of the rape of a white woman. From the same balcony as Jean Louise, Miss Lee had watched her father, Amasa Lee, defend many a case. In Florence the courthouse, bordered by gnarled mulberry trees, is the setting for the opening chapters of *The Store;* here Governor Terry O'Shawn, former Florence lawyer, conducts a late summer rally for the candidacy of Grover Cleveland. Elevated "on the portico of the courthouse in the light of four oil lamps," the orator proclaims himself "a herald of a great Democrat and a great friend of the South." The final scene of the novel is also set on Courthouse Square. Colonel Vaiden "headed the stumbling mules into the Square. The crows swarmed around the gnarled mulberries along Intelligence Row. On three of these trees, in the center of the mob, swung three figures."

The oracles and keepers of local consciences in both towns are the editors of the newspapers: *The Florence Index* is owned and run by A. Gray Lacefield, scion of a family that once possessed a great plantation; in Maycomb Mr. Underwood, who lives across from the courthouse in rooms over his printing press, "had no use for any organization but *The Maycomb Tribune,* of which he was sole owner, editor, and printer." In both towns the social and spiritual life of Negroes and whites centers in churches. As for the whites, the Vaidens have changed their religion with the generations: old Simeon Vaiden of South Carolina had been converted to Methodism by Wesley himself, and his own son Jimmie was a hardshell Alabama Baptist, and his sons, Augustus and Miltiades, are Christian Campbellites. On a Sunday morning in 1884 in the bare interior, where his wife is the song leader without benefit of instrumental music, Augustus' mind follows the fortunes of a fly caught in a spider web; "he wondered if he had taken the hog its slop that morning." In Maycomb Auntie entertains her missionary circle, which always studies the Mrunas in darkest Africa, with elaborate refreshments of coffee, charlotte, and dewberry tarts. When Mr. Finch is attending the legislature in Montgomery, Calpurnia, the cook, takes the children to church with her. Here they make some marvelous discoveries: the Rev. Sykes locks the doors until the collection reaches the proper total to relieve the distress of Sister Robinson, and Zeebo, Calpurnia's son, lines out the hymns.

> "Yeah, it's called linin'. They've done it that way as long as I can remember."
> Jem said it looked like they could save the collection money for a year and get some hymn-books.
> Calpurnia laughed. "Wouldn't do any good," she said. They can't read . . . . Can't but about four folks in First Purchase read . . . . I'm one of 'em."

Both communities have an interest in their educational institutions. Jean Louise, known to all as Scout, begins the first grade in Maycomb's public schools. Since Miss Caroline is a new teacher and from Winston County in north Alabama, which "in 1861 . . . seceded from Alabama," she must be educated about the social strata of Maycomb. After she has been shocked by the dirt and cooties of Burris Ewell, Little Chuck Little, a perennial first-grader, comforts her: "Now don't you be afraid, you just go back to your desk and teach us some more." Scout learns to her consternation that she is not yet ready to read, though she has long enjoyed the *Mobile Register* while sitting in her father's lap in the evenings; she must also stop the writing Calpurnia has taught her on rainy days: "We don't write in the first grade, we print."

Miltiades Vaiden's nephew Jerry Catlin has come to Florence from his home in Tennessee to attend the Normal School, just as young Stribling did at the turn of the century.

Jerry, who has been reading Ingersoll, refuses to attend compulsory chapel and learns some of the social cruelties operative on a small campus when Florence opinion reacts unfavorably to his uncle's cotton theft.

It is already apparent that the two novels concern family life. The Vaiden place, with its large log house near Connor's Landing and Waterloo, is presided over by Miltiades' spinster sister Cassandra, now that Augustus and Miltiades have moved to Florence, Marcia to Tennessee, Sylvester to Arkansas, and Lycurgus to Louisiana, Polycarp having died in 1865. But memories of old man Jimmie Vaiden and his forge still linger. In *Mockingbird* the home plantation at Finch's Landing on the Alabama is now run by Atticus's sister Alexandra and her husband. Memories of the family founder, old Simon Finch, the apothecary from Cornwall who had practiced medicine in Saint Stephens, still haunt the children's minds when they return to the Landing at Christmas. The mature Jean Louise, who is the story's narrator, now believes that everything goes back to Andrew Jackson, because if he "hadn't run the Creeks up the creek, Simon Finch would never have paddled up the Alabama." Though *Mockingbird* is involved with fewer characters and is not a part of a trilogy like *The Store,* it too conveys a sense of the family generations of the past.

Both T.S. Stribling and Harper Lee studied law at the University of Alabama, and Stribling practiced a few years in Florence. For this reason as well as for the excitement inherent in the American legal system where a trial, unlike the European system, is a kind of contest with the judge as referee, both of these novels take on a heightened interest at the prospect of legal action. Jem and Scout in *Mockingbird,* being children of a lawyer whose wife has been dead some time, manifest great enthusiasm for courts of law and principles of justice; Scout requires a legal explanation of the Alabama concept of rape, and Jem learns to read his father's face in the courtroom. Both children know that Tom

Robinson has been condemned when they see the jury file in and never once look Tom in the eye. But without question Atticus's defense of Tom is a challenging appeal to all that is noble and right. The Negroes who sit in the courtroom balcony pay him the silent tribute of standing as he leaves the room. Scout, who has fallen asleep after she and Jem slipped up to the colored balcony, is awakened by the Rev. Sykes, "Miss Jean Louise, stand up. Your father's passin'."

The Store is complicated with many legal entanglements. The merchant J. Handback took in twenty-five bales of cotton from the Vaidens in 1865 on the very day he sought refuge in bankruptcy. Colonel Miltiades, after he had gained the confidence of the merchant in 1884, appropriates five hundred bales and sends them down the Tennessee to New Orleans via Cairo to collect his debt, rationalizing about the value of cotton in 1865 and the interest he would have made on such a fortune during the intervening years. The Colonel is brought to court for disturbing the peace when he and Handback fight over the matter, but the case becomes highly involved when Handback and the sheriff search his house for the money without due process and thereby cause his wife Ponny, who knows nothing of these complicated affairs, to give premature birth to a child and die. Finally on the day of the Presidential election, the Colonel agrees to pay the Handbacks $10,000 as "their full legal residue in the proceeds of said cotton [$48,751.37]"; in return they will not proceed with a criminal prosecution against him lest he counter with a suit involving search without warrant and maluse. All of these technicalities are encouraged by Mr. Sandusky, a young man who reads law in Governor O'Shawn's office and boards at Augustus Vaiden's.

The final episode of the novel that leads indirectly to Toussaint's lynching is caused by another legal tangle over the loss of a deed to the Lacefield plantation that forces the Colonel to sell the mules and farm implements of his Negro sharecroppers. But Toussaint Vaiden, descended from the

Negro stock on the old Vaiden place, is urged to legal recourse by his "educated" wife Lucy and goes to court on the premise of a breach of the contract to see him through the present cotton-growing season. The case goes before Judge Abernathy's chancery court with Toussaint being represented by the opportunist Sandusky, and Miltiades by the Governor himself, who says: "I consider this case so important, so constructive, so grave that it falls under the head of state papers, gentlemen. I will stop this kind of petty persecution of white landowners by Negro tenants permanently, I trust."

Not only do these novels reach climaxes in courtroom scenes; both contain characters involved in state politics and government. Atticus Finch is a state legislator: he is always reelected without opposition even though Maycomb County disapproves some of his forward-looking concepts of justice. He is the Governor's chief support during some of the emergency sessions of the depression when "there were sit-down strikes in Birmingham; bread lines in the cities grew longer, people in the county grew poorer." In *The Store* Gracie, a mulatto half-sister of Miltiades, is the mistress of the Reconstruction Governor Beekman and lives briefly in the Governor's mansion in Montgomery. When Governor O'Shawn fails to persuade the mob from their lynching, he obtains a reprieve until the four-o'clock train can take him out of Florence before the lynching occurs, thus leaving his reputation untarnished.

It is already evident from the incidents cited that Negroes play considerable roles in both novels. Calpurnia in *Mockingbird* and Gracie in *The Store* are fully developed characters. Both have long been associated with their respective white families, and both have been taught to read and write. Calpurnia is servant as well as mother to Jean Louise, who is given moral precepts whenever she asks questions like, "Why do you talk nigger-talk to the—to your folks when you know it's not right?" Cal replies: "It's right hard to say . . . .

It's not necessary to tell all you know. It's not ladylike—in the second place, folks don't like to have somebody around knowin' more than they do."

Gracie has intuitive instincts and deep loyalties to the Vaiden family. When she is entrusted with the Colonel's $48,000 to hide from J. Handback, who comes to visit her on Saturday nights, she never hesitates nor does she question the Colonel's motives.

Negro characters also play minor roles in both novels. Zeebo, the town garbage collector, and the Rev. Sykes in *Mockingbird*—Fo' Spot, the river roustabout, and the Rev. Lump Mobray in *The Store*—are examples. In the latter Tony, Gracie's neighbor, exercises her motherly instincts as well as the small means available to her for getting her children trained for life. After her daughter Pammy Lee is suspected of becoming too familiar with young Jerry at Miss Drusilla's where she works, Tony admonishes:

> "Well, you ain't goin' back to Miss Drusilla's no mo' aftah this, Pammy Lee . . . . you's a woman now. You's worth mo'n fifty cents a week. I'm gwi' sta't out in de mownin', lookin' fuh a place wid mo' pay fuh you. I'se gwi' send Jinny Lou up to Miss Dru's in yo' place . . . an' let huh lea'n [her] to cook."

The poor whites who are either tenant farmers or ne'er-do-wells are usually jealous of the industrious Negroes near them. In both novels these men are the actual villains. It is true that the Colonel in *The Store* opposes "educating niggers" and that he treats them like children—his own children whom he can command at will—but he does not cheat them, short change them, and abuse them as does J. Handback. The merchant, however, is not overtly cruel as is Cady, the ignorant, shiftless sharecropper who burns the little Negro schoolhouse and leads the mob in lynching Toussaint. Ewell, who lives near the town dump in Maycomb, is the same type of character; he is frustrated by a decent Negro like Tom Robinson, and he forces his daughter Mayella to swear to lies, just as Cady forces his wife and daughter to support him in his feud against Toussaint. And this bottom rail of Southern society goes to even greater lengths of hate in both novels. Ewell finally tries to murder Atticus's children on a dark Halloween night, but he is prevented by Boo Radley, who happens to be lurking in the shadows. The Cadys in 1885 are more successful: they burn and lynch, and in the sequel, *Unfinished Cathedral,* it is Cady's son who dynamites part of that structure that kills Miltiades.

Because Maycomb was a "tired old town" in 1932 with its "streets turned to red slop" in rainy weather with "grass . . . on the sidewalks," its outlook and social patterns seem little different from Florence of 1884. These were times of "vague optimism": "Maycomb County had recently been told that it had nothing to fear but fear itself." Something of the same tone pervaded Florence a half century earlier: many believed that "we're going to have a period of fine business" under Cleveland, that "great Democrat and great friend of the South." For this reason the background of the two novels seems quite similar. True, the fashionable "hug-me-tight" buggy of J. Handback had given way to Maycomb's Fords and Chevrolets; an alert, respected citizen with a little innocent help from his daughter could stop a lynching in 1935, when a Governor could not in 1885. But the fate of the Negro in each case was death: the South moved slowly.

Despite this similarity of small-town background *The Store* and *To Kill a Mockingbird* are quite different books. In *The Store,* according to the publishers, Doubleday, Doran, and Company, "Mr. Stribling took upon himself the task of painting a real picture of the South, and the North as it influenced the South, precisely as all these different forces were, and not as one might wish them to be." The novel is the middle member of a trilogy concerned with "Family History and the Destiny of a Nation," the other two being

The Forge (the Vaidens during the Civil War) and *Unfinished Cathedral* (Miltiades as a wealthy twentieth-century banker). As Stribling himself has stated, his aim in the novels was historical: "Each generation quickly and completely forgets its forebears. I was filled with a profound sense of tragedy that my own family, my neighbors, the whole South surrounding me would be utterly lost in the onrushing flood of years. History will not rescue it from oblivion because history is too general to be human and too remote to be real."

To achieve so large a tapestry Stribling resorts to a heavily plotted novel. There are at least three separate, ingeniously dovetailed, struggles in *The Store*. The central plot belongs to Miltiades: his efforts to own a store like Handback's so that he may control plantations and sharecroppers, and thus restore a way of life that existed before the war. And in order to achieve this end he must have an ante-bellum home and an aristocratic wife. Though Miltiades succeeds relatively soon in breaking Handback's prowess by his bold cotton theft and public rationalization of collecting an old debt, his success leads him to the same sort of land-poor tyranny that Handback suffered, and it is not until the very end of the novel that the Colonel is accidentally saved from financial ruin, from the machinations of Handback's son, and from Sandusky's litigious subterfuges by the sudden discovery of the actual deeds that give him clear title to the Lacefield place.

To provide the proper setting for his financial comeback the Colonel seeks to marry his old sweetheart, Drusilla Lacefield Crowninshield, who jilted him before the war. Believing that Miltiades never really loved her so much as he loved the Lacefield name and that her daughter Sydna cherishes a kind of father-lover image in Miltiades, Drusilla refuses him. Nevertheless, the Colonel marries Sydna instead of her mother, and he sets about replacing the old square wooden columns on the Crowninshield "manor" with round stone ones.

The second plot belongs to Gracie, the mulatto half-sister of the Colonel, who is also the mother of his son Toussaint, whom the Colonel believes is the illegitimate son of the carpet-bag Governor Beekman. She is also the mistress of J. Handback, who has built her the little house in East Florence that he visits regularly. Gracie's loyalties are torn between family ties to the Vaidens and gratitude to Handback, who ultimately offers her marriage and escape to Louisiana, where she and Toussaint can pass as French or Caribbean. When she refuses because she has been too much involved with Miltiades' cotton theft, she foregoes her life-long wish to find a way to educate Toussaint and to take him out of a Negro environment. Handback commits suicide, but Gracie goes on struggling. Toussaint marries Lucy Lacefield, an "educated" Negro girl whose parents still live on the old Lacefield place; Gracie is installed by Miltiades in the Lacefield manor house where she, Toussaint, and Lucy farm on shares. At last their struggle with the Negro-hating Cady leads indirectly to Toussaint's suing Miltiades and the subsequent lynching, after which Gracie and Lucy flee north to the Ohio on the *Rapidan,* aided by Fo' Spot, who is rousting on the boat.

Nor is this all. A third plot belongs to Miltiades' nephew Jerry, who reads Ingersoll and studies Yoga: he is in love with Sydna Crowninshield, a few years his senior. His struggles to express his love as well as to maintain his anti-religious convictions at Florence Normal mark him a Vaiden. His roommate at Mrs. Rose Vaiden's boarding-house is O'Shawn's law clerk, Sandusky, whose rabid pursuit of legal complications links Jerry with all the other plots of the novel.

It has been necessary to outline these plots in order to demonstrate that even in a novel of 571 closely printed pages little additional action can be compressed within its scope. Stribling has always been skillful in designing and interweaving patterns of struggle. His long interest in adventure and detective fiction is evident. Even in his serious novels that preceded *The Store* Stribling uses many of the features dear to nineteenth-century novelists: withholding of relevant information until a more dramatic moment, designing "teasers" to entice the reader to the next chapter, and straining probability in the attempt to enmesh plot within plot. Such devices usually succeed with a first reading, but for the second they impede as well as reveal other weaknesses.

The chief of these—often the fault of all but the best historical fiction—is the lack of character motivation. Despite the numerous characters in *The Store,* only two are well drawn, Miltiades and Gracie. The others are interesting, at times vivid and picturesque, pathetic or amusing, but they are painted paper and cannot be turned sideways, cannot be questioned. Enough has already been said about Gracie and Miltiades to suggest the variety of situations they find themselves in. Though they seem living people whose problems can be vicariously shared, their motives for action are not always clear. An example at the beginning and end of the novel will illustrate this contention. When J. Handback mistakes Miltiades for the hardware drummer Bivins after Governor O'Shawn's speech for Cleveland, he asks the Colonel if he would mind delivering a message to Bivins at the hotel. When the Colonel inquires why he doesn't deliver it himself, Handback replies that Bivins would try to sell him more items than he needs. Apparently satisfied with this explanation from his old enemy, Miltiades agrees, and from this slim thread of a beginning the Colonel gains a position in Handback's store, steals his cotton and ultimately wrecks the merchant. This action on the part of both men who mortally hate each other is highly improbable. Since both have a sardonic fear of each other, the more one sees of their subsequent actions the less likely does he feel that either man would have been motivated to react in this way at this moment.

At the end of the novel, Gracie, who has always wanted to take Toussaint out of the Deep South and has never liked the idea of his marriage to the Negro Lucy, leaves on the *Rapidan* with her. Why we are never told. Gracie's journey is apparently financed by Fo' Spot, a Negro she never cared for. The reader is left to supply whatever motivation he can come by. Perhaps her deep grief for Toussaint is enough to drive her away. But Gracie never acts impulsively, and the terrifying final scene is almost ruined by this tag end of unmotivated action.

The host of minor characters in the novel—Landers, the Republican postmaster; Ponny, Miltiades' first wife; Captain Dargan of the *Zebulon D;* Bradley, the real estate agent; and Negroes like Andy, the porter at the Florence Hotel—are vivid and momentarily convincing. Stribling's ability to sketch a portrait in brief dialogue and pictorial gesture is impressive. But the lack of motivation for his main characters is often hidden behind this gallery of minor portraits and the onrush of events.

Perhaps his concern with the complexities of action also betrays Stribling in the realm of ideas just as it does in his character motivation. Robert Penn Warren in an essay, "T.S. Stribling: a Paragraph in the History of Critical Realism," points out that when this novelist turns from the contemporary to the historical scene, he brings along with him his same set of ideas and his same concepts of sociology. "For him almost any young white man who does not live in a large city is a hobbledehoy," like Jerry Catlin. Religion is a somewhat "greasy" affair; "it is impossible for a person to be devout without, at the same time, being a fool," like Augustus Vaiden and his pious, fussy wife Rose. In regard to race Stribling always brings "into collusion a noble Negro, or rather a mixed-breed, and a white society considerably less than noble." This is the theme of *Birthright,* dealing with a Harvard-educated Negro who returns to his native Tennessee, and it is a theme of *The Store,* dealing with Gracie, Toussaint, and Lucy.

There is nothing wrong with the thematic idea—it is surely a valid one—but Stribling in isolating it for examination glosses over the basic historical situation in the South of 1884: the real problems of how to handle the franchise, how to solve the shift in the labor scene, or how to replace the social pattern of the plantation. It is true that *The Store* touches on these issues, but always to the same purpose: except for a brutality and stupidity peculiar to the Southern white man, Stribling would have us believe that all these problems would have been solved long ago. A city, preferably a northern one, would immediately save Jerry from being a country hick, and there Toussaint and Gracie would already have been free and equal. In Stribling's pantheon there are no equitable Southern white men. They are all rather like J. Handback, who believes that a pound for a nigger is twelve ounces, or like Miltiades Vaiden, who would prolong the peonage of the plantation through the benign dictatorship of the store.

In other words, Stribling vitiates much of his fictional validity because he bends his characters to fit his ideas, and for this reason they never seem properly real. Stribling had read his V.L. Parrington, H.L. Mencken, and Sinclair Lewis too uncritically. Or, to put the matter another way, he reflects too unquestioningly the prevailing attitude of American liberalism of the 1920's.

Two additional traits combine in *The Store* to make it seem brittle and superficial. The point of view is nowhere artistically useful, and the style is often a kind of hasty journalese. Basically the omniscient perspective controls his narrative, but Stribling's delight in the short paragraph and pointed dialogue plunges the reader into an immediacy that is jarringly broken with regularity. When Miltiades rushes to Gracie's house to rescue his $48,000, he discovers that $300 is missing.

> "What did you take it for?" trembled the Colonel.
> "For—for Miss Ponny, Colonel Milt," breathed the woman.
> "Ponny! Ponny! What did Ponny want with three . . ."
> "Oh Mas' Milt!" gasped Gracie, "to buy a coffin . . . to buy a

coffin for her and her little baby . . . ."

And the quadroon began weeping, with a faint gasping sound, battling against her emotions like a white woman.

No valid objection can be made to the omniscient perspective, long a favorite with generations of storytellers. Sinclair Lewis, Stribling's mentor, often uses it with striking effect as in *Babbitt* where he begins a series of sections with the phrase, "At this moment in Zenith . . . ." The trouble with Stribling's use of the perspective is that he wants the best of the two worlds of god-like omniscience and of first-person immediacy both at the same time.

Despite these faults that doubtless seem more obvious today than in the rather lean literary years of the early 1930's, *The Store* has a certain enduring vitality. In addition to a galloping narrative that does not entirely bolt into bypaths of improbabilities as is the case with *Unfinished Cathedral,* the novel has many moments that preserve the way of small-town life in Alabama and at the same time explicate a thematic concept. When Sydna is discussing the difficulty of understanding northerners, she says:

"I can't possibly understand the taste of Yankees."

"Why, darling, of course you can't," agreed Drusilla; "they're tradespeople."

"Mother . . . Colonel Milt runs a store!"

"My dear, Miltiades has to run a store to keep his business going. It's not because he wants to run a store . . . . By the way, have you ever been in his store, Sydna?"

"No, I haven't."

"Well, it's a sight, and I consider that a great honor to the keeper, because it shows that he doesn't care a thing in the world about the store as a store."

When Stribling wrote *The Store,* he was fifty; he had taught school, practiced law, traveled widely, worked on several newspapers and magazines; he had written quantities of journalistic material, adventure stories, detective fiction, and at least five novels that had received considerable critical attention: *Birthright* (1922), *Teeftallow* (1926), *Bright Metal* (1928), *Backwater* (1930), and *The Forge* (1931). When Harper Lee wrote *To Kill a Mockingbird,* she was in her early thirties; she had studied law at the University of Alabama, worked in the reservation department of an international airline, and spent most of her time in New York recollecting the South and learning to write. She had worked hard on her first novel, which was some three years "churning through the editorial mills of the house of Lippincott," reported *News-Week.* The aspiring author had quit her desk job and "hived up" in a cold-water flat. The result is a remarkable achievement.

One of the things about Stribling that disturbed Robert Penn Warren in 1934 when he was writing about the new Pulitzer Prize winner was that the author "has never been interested in the dramatic possibilities of a superior white man brought into conflict with his native environment," a matter that has challenged many serious Southern novelists like William Faulkner and Caroline Gordon. A quarter of a century later Miss Lee has done precisely that for the Alabama scene. Even though it is usually easier to write about the spectacular, wicked man, Miss Lee has chosen the more difficult task of writing about the quiet, good man. Other novelists have been concerned with this type of man— the thoughtful, well-educated Southerner at quiet odds with his environment like the minor character Gavin Stevens in Faulkner's *Intruder in the Dust.* But Miss Lee has made him the central figure and hero of her novel and succeeded at the same time in writing an exciting and significant story.

The epigraph from Charles Lamb—"Lawyers, I suppose, were once children''—indicates the two aspects of *Mockingbird,* childhood and the law. The plot can be simply stated: Atticus Finch, one of Maycomb's leading attorneys, is the court-appointed defender of Tom Robinson, accused of raping Mayella Ewell, a daughter of the town's notorious poor white-trash family. In this struggle he is unsuccessful—at least the all-white jury finds Tom guilty, and he is killed escaping from prison before Atticus can gain a hearing on the appeal. But to a certain extent the case is not altogether lost; certain precedents have been set. Instead of a young lawyer who defends only for the record's sake Judge Taylor appoints a distinguished lawyer who chooses to fight obvious lies and racial hatred so that he and his children—and ultimately Maycomb itself—can remain honest and honorable people. No one except Atticus Finch ever kept a jury out so long on a case involving a Negro. And in the process of the trial Atticus's children have matured in the right way—at least in his eyes.

The struggle of the children toward maturity, however, occupies more space than Atticus's struggle to free Tom, the central episode. Through their escapades and subsequent entanglements with their father and neighbors like Miss Maudie Atkinson, Mrs. Henry Lafayette Dubose, and particularly the legends about Boo Radley, the town's boogie man, Jem and Scout learn what it means to come to man's estate. In Part I, an evocation of the happy days of summer play, the process is begun. With their friend Dill Harris from Meridian they enact the weird stories about Boo Radley— how he sits in his shuttered house all day and wanders about in the shadows of night looking in people's windows, how he once drove the scissors into his father's leg, how as a not-too-bright adolescent he had terrorized the county with a "gang" from Old Sarum. Might he even be dead in that solemn, silent house, the children wonder. Miss Maudie gives, as always, a forthright answer to that question: "I know he's alive, Jean Louise, because I haven't seen him carried out yet." Although Atticus forbids these "Boo Radley" games, the children go on playing—Scout being Mrs. Radley, who sweeps the porch and screams that Arthur (Boo's real name) is murdering them all with the scissors, Dill being old Mr. Radley, who walks silently down the street and coughs whenever he is spoken to, and Jem being the star actor, Boo himself as "he went under the front steps and shrieked and howled from time to time."

In the midst of these juvenile Gothic masques the children begin to learn something about the difference between gossip and truth. When Jem tears his pants and is forced to leave them behind on the wire fence during their night expedition to peek through the Radleys' shutters, he later finds them crudely mended, pressed, and hanging over the fence. When Miss Maudie's house burns during a cold night, all the neighborhood turns out to help and to watch. Scout, who is told to come no closer than the Radleys' gate, discovers that during the confusion a blanket has been thrown round her shoulders. Jem realizes that this thoughtful act was not performed by Mr. or Mrs. Radley, who have long been dead, and he saw Mr. Nathan, Boo's brother and "jailer," helping haul out Miss Maudie's mattress. It could have been only Boo.

One of the most interesting features of *Mockingbird* is the skill with which Miss Lee weaves these two struggles about childhood and the law together into one thematic idea. Like Stribling she does a neat workmanlike job of dovetailing her plots. When Scout attends her first day at school, the morning session is devoted to explaining the Cunningham family to Miss Caroline so that she will understand why she must not lend Walter any lunch money. The Cunninghams are poor but proud. When the Sunday night lynching party arrives at the jail, it is Jem and Scout, who, having slipped off from home, see their father calmly reading a newspaper by the light at the jail door, sitting in one of his office chairs. Hiding in the doorway of the Jitney Jungle, Scout rushes forward in time to disconcert the Cunningham mob by asking innocent questions about Walter, her classmate—her father had always taught her to talk to folks about the things that would interest them.

The afternoon session of Scout's first day at school had been taken up with Burris Ewell and his dirt and defiance of

Miss Caroline. It is Burris's father who brings the charge of rape against Tom Robinson.

This neatness that makes for economy of character portrayal is successful when it avoids the appearance of too convenient coincidental circumstances—a fault that *Mockingbird* does not entirely escape. But in the more important aspect of thematic development the novel is successful. Carson McCullers and Truman Capote have written with insight about Southern childhood, and William Faulkner has traced the legal and moral injustices done the Negro just as Eudora Welty has underlined the quiet patience of the Negro's acceptance of his bleak world. Harper Lee has united these two concepts into the image of a little child—schooled in basic decencies by her father even though "ladylike" manners of the superficial sort that Aunt Alexandra admires are sometimes lacking—who turns the tide to stop the Sunday night lynching. After the trial when Jem cannot comprehend the injustice done Tom Robinson by the jury, he asks his father, "How could they do it, how could they?" Atticus replies, "I don't know, but they did it. They've done it before and they did it tonight and they'll do it again and when they do it—seems that only the children weep."

Almost all readers will agree that the first two-thirds of *Mockingbird* is excellent fiction; the difference of opinion will probably turn upon the events after the trial. The major incident here is the school pageant about the history of Maycomb County as written by Mrs. Merriweather; the performance is the town's attempt at "organized activity" on Halloween. On their way home from the pageant, Ewell attacks the Finch children to get even with Atticus for making him appear a complete and guilty fool at Tom's trial. Scout is saved from the knife by her wire costume representing a Maycomb County ham; Jem receives a painful broken arm. And Ewell is killed with his own knife by Boo Radley, who again lurks opportunely in the shadows. Later that night after visits from the doctor and the sheriff when Scout is allowed to walk home with Mr. Arthur, she stands for a moment on the Radley porch seeing the knothole in the tree where Boo had once left them pitiful little presents of chewing gum and Indian-head pennies. She half realizes as a child of nine, and now as an adult she more fully realizes, what their childish antics must have meant to a lonely, "imprisoned," mentally limited man like Mr. Arthur, and she recalls her father's word to Jem that "you never really know a man until you *stand* in his shoes and walk around in them. Just standing on the Radley porch was enough."

Thematically the aftermath of the injustice done Tom and the growing up of a boy and girl are brought together in the Halloween episode. The structural problem of joining Boo Radley and Tom Robinson into some sort of juxtaposition is solved, but the slapstick comedy of the school pageant and the grotesque coincidental tragedy and subsequent salvation are perilously close to the verge of melodrama—the same sort of melodrama that blights the novels of Stribling. To keep this section of *Mockingbird* from seeming altogether an anticlimax to the trial of Tom, it should at least have been denominated Part III. Then the story would have been set off into its three components of School and Summer Play, Tom Robinson's Trial, and Halloween Masquerade. Such a device would distribute the thirty-one chapters into the equal grouping of Miss Lee's apparent planning, and at the same time it would not force the Halloween tragi-comedy to seem quite so close to the climactic trial.

It is strange that the structural *forte* of *Mockingbird*, the point of view of the telling, is either misunderstood or misinterpreted by most of the initial reviewers of the novel. Phoebe Adams in the *Atlantic Monthly* calls it "frankly and completely impossible, being told in the first person by a six-year-old girl with the prose and style of a well-educated adult." Richard Sullivan in the *Chicago Tribune* is puzzled and only half understands: "The unaffected young narrator uses adult language to render the matter she deals with, but the point of view is cunningly restricted to that of a perceptive, independent child, who doesn't always understand fully what's happening, but who conveys completely, by implication, the weight and burden of the story." More careful reviewers like Granville Hicks in the *Saturday Review* and F.H. Lyell in the *New York Times* are more perceptive. The latter states the matter neatly: "Scout is the narrator, reflecting in maturity on childhood events of the mid-Thirties."

Maycomb and the South, then, are all seen through the eyes of Jean Louise, who speaks from the mature and witty vantage of an older woman recalling her father as well as her brother and their childhood days. This method is managed with so little ado that the average reader slips well into the story before he realizes that the best evidence that Atticus has reared an intellectually sophisticated daughter is that she remembers her formative years in significant detail and then narrates them with charm and wisdom. She has become the good daughter of a good man, who never let his children know what an expert marksman he was until he was forced to kill a mad dog on their street. Atticus did not like to shoot for the mere sport of it lest he kill a mockingbird like Tom Robinson or Boo Radley; and mockingbirds must be protected for their songs' sake.

This modification of a Jamesian technique of allowing the story to be seen only through the eyes of a main character but to be understood by the omniscient intelligence of Henry James is here exploited to bold advantage. The reader comes to learn the true meaning of Maycomb through the eyes of a child who now recollects with the wisdom of maturity. Along with Scout and Jem we may at first be puzzled why Atticus insists that Jem read every afternoon to old Mrs. Henry Lafayette Dubose in atonement for his cutting the tops off her camellia bushes after she taunted him about his father's being "no better than the niggers and trash he works for."

But we soon learn with Scout that Atticus believed Jem would become aware of the real meaning of courage when he was forced to aid a dying old woman in breaking the narcotic habit she abhorred.

Jean Louise's evolving perception of the social milieu in her home town as she grows up in it and as she recalls her own growing up involves the reader in an understanding of the various strata of Maycomb society and its Southern significance. After Jem has brooded about the trial, he explains to Scout that

> There's four kinds of folks in the world. There's the ordinary kind like us and the neighbors, there's the kind like the Cunninghams out in the woods, the kind like the Ewells down at the dump, and the Negroes.
> "What about the Chinese, and the Cajuns down yonder in Baldwin County?"
> "I mean in Maycomb County. The thing about it is, our kind of folks don't like the Cunninghams, and the Cunninghams don't like the Ewells, and the Ewells hate and despise the colored folks."
> I told Jem if that was so, then why didn't Tom's jury, made up of folks like the Cunninghams, acquit Tom to spite the Ewells?

After considerable debate Scout concludes, "Naw, Jem, I think there's just one kind of folks. Folks."

This naively sophisticated sociological rationalization is far more valid and persuasive in its two-pronged approach. As mature readers we realize its mature validity; as observers of children we delight in their alert reactions to the unfolding events. The convolutions of the "mind of Henry James" have given way to the immediacy and pithy wisdom of Jean Louise's first-person narration.

Though Miss Lee may not have solved all her problems of style in the dual approach of child eyes and mature heart, *Mockingbird* demonstrates the powerful effect and economy of a well-conceived point of view as opposed to the discursive, shifting omniscience of *The Store.* With the passage of years from 1933 to 1961 James, Joyce, and Faulkner have been archetypical in shaping perspectives for both writers and readers of fiction. Neither Harper Lee nor T.S. Stribling is a novelist of innovations. Stribling borrows heavily from the popular methods of Lewis and Hergesheimer, and creates in *The Store* an Alabama panorama, lusty and lurid, of the 1880's. Superficial in its sociology as well as in its narrative techniques, it nevertheless demonstrates the virile power of the tale of action in a wealth of realistic background of gaslight, carriages, and pistols. In the same year as *The Store* Faulkner published *Light in August,* also the story of a man of mixed breed in conflict with the thoughtful and thoughtless society around him. Faulkner has shown the way for Southern fiction to grapple with its deep problems of race conflict. And William March later in the 1930's and the 1940's has called attention on the Alabama scene to the whole untapped reservoir of the average man—the shopkeepers and farmers around Reedyville—the people "like us," as Jem says.

Miss Lee, in a sense, has actually revealed more of Alabama history from the Simon Finches of old Saint Stephens to distrusted Republicans like the Misses Barber from Clanton than does Stribling in his much longer historical novel. The spirit of history is as important as the events of history, and Miss Lee presents Miss Caroline as an outsider from Winston County because she represents to this Maycomb community what every South Alabama child knew about north Alabama: a place "full of Liquor Interests, Big Mules, steel companies, Republicans, professors, and other persons of no background." Miss Lee has mastered an eclectic technique of a meaningful point of view along with validity of idea and freshness of material. She echoes Faulkner in her deep concern for the inchoate tragedy of the South, and like him she is not afraid to pursue the Gothic shadows of Edgar Allan Poe. But her eclecticism is her own: she has told a story of racial injustice from the point of view of thoughtful children with "open, unprejudiced, well-furnished minds of their own," as the *New York Times* has phrased it. And in Atticus Finch she has created the most memorable portrait in recent fiction of the just and equitable Southern liberal.

The symbols of *store* and *mockingbird* are true symbols of the South. The economy of the plantations was swallowed up in the economy of the store. But Timrod's mockingbird, creature of the strong and gentle song that rightly heard can save the land from its inbred violence, is a symbol at once more profound and poignant.

2

Alabama Geography in Shirley Ann Grau's The Keepers of the House

WITH the awarding of the 1964 Pulitzer Prize for fiction to *The Keepers of the House,* Shirley Ann Grau takes her place as a major Southern novelist. Previously she had published only two other novels, *The Hard Blue Sky* (1958) and *The House on Coliseum Street* (1961), and numerous short stories, some of which she collected in her first book, *The Black Prince and Other Stories* (1955).

Like every good novelist Miss Grau is more than a regional writer. Her characters transcend their surroundings just as her novels are significant beyond the stories themselves. In *The Keepers of the House,* however, she has a special geographical problem worthy of special analysis. Her approach toward a solution demonstrates a part of her skill as a fictional historian who is also a first-rate novelist. To achieve fictional reality almost every novelist creates a unique time and place for his characters to inhabit. To underscore his right to this privilege many a novelist has even created a whole fictional region or county that can become his sole property, which may be "like" an actual region without being that region. Thus Trollope devised his Barsetshire, Hardy his Wessex, and Faulkner his Yoknapatawpha.

In similar fashion Shirley Ann Grau has devised for *The Keepers of the House* a Wade County with Madison City its county seat. And like Faulkner she has sketched the regional history even to Indian days, for her story recounts the struggles of the generations who have been the builders and keepers of a house on the banks of the Providence River that flows down to Mobile. In her novel Miss Grau must make her setting representative of the Alabama-Mississippi-Louisiana area because she is concerned with Deep South race relations, particularly with miscegenation and its effect on later generations and finally on the wife of a candidate for the governorship of the state. However, since the sweep of these events naturally touches upon a state history in general and contemporary politics in particular, Miss Grau would prefer to intimate the locality of the region without actually naming the state. She cannot find so easy a solution as did William March when he wrote in the 1930's and 1940's about a similar county between Montgomery and Mobile. His Pearl County with Reedyville its county seat is admittedly in Alabama, with March—like Faulkner—its "sole owner and proprietor." This setting serves March well for numerous short stories and for novels like *The Tallons* and *The Looking-Glass,* which turn upon timeless kinds of character rather than upon political events in Alabama. By the very nature of its themes March's fiction takes on a broad connotation; Reedyville itself could be the county seat of almost any Southern county.

Like March's novels, Harper Lee's *To Kill a Mockingbird,* as discussed in the first essay, can also patently admit to an Alabama scene. The events take place in Maycomb and Maycomb County primarily from 1932 to 1935. Miss Lee locates Maycomb "some twenty miles east of Finch's Landing . . . on the banks of the Alabama River." Since Miss Lee's novel centers around an event of local rather than state-wide significance—a Negro's alleged rape of a white woman—without becoming involved in state history she can allow Atticus Finch, the hero-lawyer, to serve in the Alabama legislature at Montgomery; but for his hometown she apparently deems it wise to create a fictitious county seat not unlike her childhood hometown of Monroeville in Monroe County. In distinct contrast Alabama is named outright by T.S. Stribling in *The Store,* the middle member of a trilogy including *The Forge* and *Unfinished Cathedral.* His problem is similar to Miss Grau's, but he chooses to designate specifically the setting for these novels: Northwest Alabama, in and around Florence. *The Forge* takes place on the farms and plantations near the Tennessee River; the opening page states: "It was thus that log houses were fashioned in Alabama, years ago, when he [old man Jimmie Vaiden] and his family and his slaves had immigrated from South Carolina." The last two novels depict life in Florence from 1884 to the 1920's. Stribling, like Miss Grau, is concerned with the governorship and state politics. Because he deals with numerous melodramatic events that he awkwardly attempts to weave into the actual tapestry of Alabama history by such devices as naming governors who never really existed, Stribling's readers doubt the validity of his entire fictional world even on a first reading.

To avoid difficulties and comparisons of this sort Miss Grau does not name the state containing Wade County. She refers to "the capital city," "the capital's evening paper," "the state university"; and near the center of the state one crosses a Red River. But such generalizations and rechristenings do not remove from the reader's intuition a feeling that this is an Alabama story. The builder and first keeper of the house, William Marshall Howland, was "from Tennessee," having marched north in 1815 after the Battle of New Orleans, just as Harper Lee's narrator-heroine remarks of her progenitor, Simon Finch, who had paddled up the Alabama River after Jackson had won that battle and had vigorously cleared the Alabama territory of Creeks. Howland did not settle in the "fat black delta land that lay to the North" but pushed on "toward the east" to a small river he named Providence in memory of his mother. The family "farmed and hunted; they made whiskey and rum and took it to market down the Providence River to Mobile." When this progenitor was murdered by the Choctaws, his neighbors "trailed the Indians to the Black Warrior River." In the later days of railroads family relatives come "over from Atlanta," passing through Opelika. In the northern section is a "TVA lake," which is popular with university students for week-end jaunts. When John Tolliver explains to his wife Abigail Howland Mason that he plans to be the state governor and later a senator, he says:

'I've been forgetting to tell you, I joined the Citizens Council and the Klan before I left Madison City.'
'Oh,' I said, 'oh, for heaven's sake.'
'Your grandfather belonged to the Klan.'
'It was different then.'
'Justice Black belonged too.'
'But not any more.'
'Honey,' he said, 'when I get where he is, I'll quit too.'

No one of these references conclusively proves "the state" to be Alabama, but the total impression strengthens that belief.

The comments of reviewers and critics about locale are varied, but they too point in an Alabama direction: "a small Southern town" *(Virginia Quarterly Review),* "a town in what seems to be southern Alabama" (Frederick C. Crews, New York *Times),* "somewhere in the Gulf Coast territory near Louisiana" (Katherine Gauss Jackson, *Harper's),* "town in Alabama" (Robert Coles, *New Republic),* "a plantation, which was staked out north of New Orleans" (Edward Weeks, *Atlantic),* and "in the southern Delta Country" (Miriam Ylvisker, *Library Journal),* "down in Gulf Coast country" *(Newsweek),* "in some unnamed state that may be Alabama" (Granville Hicks, *Saturday Review).*

This Alabama conclusion can also be tested negatively. If not Alabama, perhaps Mississippi or Louisiana would be more plausible; Georgia is not to be considered because Atlanta is always mentioned in an out-of-state context and because Madison City is in the hinterland of Mobile: an earlier generation had "hired a regular tomb builder to come from Mobile," and for the new house built in the 1950's Abigail "had a contractor from Mobile do the kitchen and the bathrooms." Louisiana is not a possibility despite the vivid swamp and bayou descriptions of the Robertsons' stills so typical of Miss Grau's Louisiana scenery in *The Hard Blue Sky.* "The state" is "mostly Baptist," it has counties instead of parishes, John Tolliver is going to build a state political machine "better than the one the Longs have in Louisiana," and Abigail is "supposed to call a man in Louisiana to say that we would buy his beautiful little roan Shetland." "The state" is not Mississippi, because during Abigail's sojourn at her state university she is expelled for helping a friend elope with a racing jockey: "Tuesday morning, nine of us—two cars full—drove to the nearest town in Mississippi."

Along with these positive and negative hints of an Alabama scene, the reader notes that the jackets of Miss Grau's books contain the comment that although born and presently living in New Orleans "she was brought up in Alabama." And readers of her earlier short stories and novels are aware that she knows the Alabama landscape well. In 'White Girl, Fine Girl," one of the stories in *The Black Prince and Other Stories,* she writes of a state capital like Montgomery that she calls Stanhope: "You can't see Kilby [Prison] from any point inside the limits of Stanhope, though if you stood on the capitol steps, on the spot where Jeff Davis took his first oath, you'd be staring in the right direction . . . ." In "Joshua," another story from the same volume, Miss Grau transfers the name of the quaint little Alabama fishing port of Bon Secour in Baldwin County to Louisiana:

South of New Orleans, down along the stretch that is called the Lower Coast . . . Joshua Samuel Watkins sat at the kitchen table

in one of the dozen-odd houses that make up Bon Secour, Good
Hope, the farthest of the towns along the dirt highway, which
ends there, and the nearest town to the river's mouth.

In *The House on Coliseum Street,* which takes place
chiefly in New Orleans, Joan's mother's second husband is a
"tall thin Lincoln-like Alabamian"; and Joan's suitor, Michael
Kern, has an aunt

'or maybe she's a great-aunt, and she lives in Montgomery . . . .
You'd like her. Nice old gal. You see her house, right up on top a
hill looking out on some other pitched roofs and cupolas all the
way down to the Alabama River. I used to wonder why they call
it a river when it's nothing more than a yellow creek full of
garbage. You know, sometimes you can smell it clear up to the
house when the wind's right in summer.'

With all of this implied background from a novelist who
knows Alabama well it may seem surprising that the word
"Alabama" does not appear in *The Keepers of the House*
until the Epilogue, where it takes on the force of a "surprise
ending" for the seemingly gradual identification of the geographical setting. After Abigail has stood off the townspeople
and county hoodlums who succeed only in burning her barn,
she visits her husband's father in the northern part of the
state to leave a message for John. "It said only that my
lawyer would get in touch with him about a property
settlement, and that I wanted him to go to Alabama for a
quick divorce." This one rapier thrust of the word
"Alabama" instead of clinching the reader's impressions
gathered from the numerous earlier descriptions of the setting succeeds in negating them all. And Miss Grau thus says
to the prying and curious that her story takes place in neither
Georgia, Mississippi, Louisiana, nor Alabama. It is of course
set in a Deep South state of mind, "the state"; for its truth as
a novel is inherent in the story itself, not in the reader's
preconceived notions about its geographical locale.

Miss Grau handles her geography adroitly and meaning-fully: she hints at Louisiana with her swamp scenes and Red River. Her North Trace, Battle of Tim's Crossing, and "Tolliver Nation" with its "northernmost county . . . [slave] breeding plantations" suggest Mississippi with its Natchez Trace, its devastating Civil War battle at Shiloh, and its northern slave-breeding counties along the Mississippi— DeSoto, Tunica, and Coahoma. The strongest and most consistent pointing is toward Alabama with many references to Mobile, Birmingham, the Black Warrior River, and to the whole history and milieu of the state. But Miss Grau denies them all by the contextual sense of the only mention of the word "Alabama." For the reader who is not keenly aware of the history and geography of the South or who expects in a novel a sociological gloss on past or current events she seems to offer a choice of states; for the historically and critically knowledgeable reader she has a gentle reminder: fiction has its own broad canvas, its own reality.

3

Alabama In The
Short Story:
Notes for an Anthology

IN the closing decades of the nineteenth century short story writers, encouraged by publishing firms, were rediscovering their local regions, now that the nation stretching from the Atlantic to the Pacific was no more a house divided. Mrs. Stowe had turned from *Uncle Tom's Cabin* to *Oldtown Fireside Stories* (1872). Many other New Englanders followed her example. In 1891 appeared Rose Terry Cooke's *Huckleberries Gathered from New England Hills;* by the end of the century Sarah Orne Jewett had created a minor masterpiece in *The Country of the Pointed Firs.*

In varying degrees and with varying success short fiction with partially realistic background developed in the South, the Middle West, and the Far West. In the South, for example, George W. Cable issued *Old Creole Days* in 1879, Mary Noailles Murfree *In the Tennessee Mountains* in 1884, Thomas Nelson Page *In Old Virginia* in 1887, and Harry Stillwell Edwards *Two Runaways and Other Stories* in 1889. James Lane Allen's *Flute and Violin,* his first Kentucky collection, appeared in 1891. At the turn of the century Will N. Harben's *Northern Georgia Sketches* and Samuel Minturn Peck's *Alabama Sketches* were continuing the tradition.

At the midpoint of the twentieth century anthologists, encouraged often by university presses, were summarizing a new aspect of the same tradition state by state. In 1940 the

Louisiana State University Press issued Lizzie Carter McVoy's *Louisiana in the Short Story,* opening with a selection from George W. Cable and closing with stories by J. Frank Dobie, Stark Young, and Elma Godchaux. In 1948 Richard Walser edited *North Carolina in the Short Story,* published by the University of North Carolina Press. In 1952 the University of South Carolina Press released Katharine M. Jones and Mary Verner Schlaefer's *South Carolina in the Short Story,* " . . . a mosaic of life in [the] state as interpreted by its own people." And in 1954 *Kentucky Story,* edited by Hollis Summers and published by the University of Kentucky Press, began with a story by James Lane Allen.

One of the chief difficulties in compiling these anthologies is that of deciding which authors are to be considered. McVoy chooses stories about Louisiana regardless of the authors' native states because so many good writers have been "attracted to Louisiana by its romantic material." Summers solves the problem by selecting stories "whose authors are Kentuckians, thirteen by accident of birth, two by deliberate adoption." Similarly the editors of the South Carolina volume have chosen stories by "native or adopted South Carolinians" but without precisely defining the terms. Such criteria, however, make for strange companions. It is disconcerting to discover Robert Penn Warren bracketed a Kentuckian along with John Fox, Jr., and Irvin S. Cobb because of "accident of birth." Far more significant portions of his life were associated with Tennessee, Louisiana, Minnesota, and Connecticut. In this day of increasing mobility, American writers are rarely associated solely or even primarily with only one state. It is rather as Professor St. Joseph remarks to the Reedyville novelist, Minnie McInnis McMinn, in the end of William March's *The Looking-Glass:* "It looks as if most of Reedyville's old citizens are living in New York now, doesn't it? Maybe that's where your book should end too. Maybe that's where all books about the South eventually end."

In fact, this observation on the mobility of people and the kaleidoscopic settings of much fiction raises the whole question of the validity of compiling or examining anthologies organized by statehood. The United States of America, however, is a large and diverse nation, and there is occasionally some justification for looking at its short fiction in geographical compartments. And what is more important: if fiction is a valid picture of some of the innumerable facets of what is called life, then occasionally it may be worthwhile to examine what sort of representation a state or region has received in the stories men have set down—regardless of where these men were born or once lived. For surely knowledge about a state is not solely to be found in encyclopedias, reports, legal documents, letters, newspapers, and what historians choose to call history. There is much wisdom in the adage that fiction is truer than fact, for fiction is broad of scope and vastly varied in content, while fact like truth is sometimes generalized and always elusive. True history embraces all the humanities.

The virtues and difficulties notwithstand, the following is a projected table of contents for an anthology of "Alabama in the Short Story." After the author and title of the stories are listed the source and year of the first major publication, the Alabama setting, and the approximate date of the events insofar as they can be determined from each story—features not generally included in the table of contents of anthologies but gathered from the stories themselves.

1. Howell Vines, "The Ginseng Gatherers" (*Southern Review,* 1936), Headwaters of the Warrior River, c. 1830
2. Johnson J. Hooper, "The Captain Attends a Camp-Meeting" (*Some Adventures of Captain Simon Suggs, Late of the Tallapoosa Volunteers; together with "Taking the Census" and Other Alabama Sketches,* 1845), Tallapoosa County near the Chambers County line, c. 1840

3. Joseph G. Baldwin, "Samuel Hele, Esquire: A Yankee School-mistress and an Alabama Lawyer" (*The Flush Times of Alabama and Mississippi: A Series of Sketches,* 1853), probably Gainesville, c. 1840

4. Ambrose Bierce, "An Occurrence at Owl Creek Bridge" (*Tales of Soldiers and Civilians,* 1891), Northern Alabama, 1864-65

5. Samuel Minturn Peck, "Pap's Mules" (*Alabama Sketches,* 1902), Oakville [Tuscaloosa], 1865

6. Howell Vines, "The Mustydines Was Ripe" (*Atlantic Monthly,* 1935), Jefferson County, 1877

7. Edgar Valentine Smith, "Prelude" (*Harper's Magazine,* 1923), probably Baldwin County, c.1900

8. William March, "Whistles" (*Good Housekeeping,* 1945), Hodgetown [Lockhart], c. 1905

9. William March, "The Little Wife" (*Midland,* 1930), Montgomery to Mobile, c. 1914

10. Edgar Valentine Smith, " 'Lijah" (*Harper's Magazine,* 1924), "Wynnesborough," near the Tombigbee River, c. 1918

11. Harriet Hassell, "History of the South" (*Story,* 1938), near Camden, c. 1920

12. Andrew Lytle, "Jericho, Jericho, Jericho" (*Southern Review,* 1936), Tennessee Valley, c. 1920

13. Robert Gibbons, "Departure of Hubbard" (*Tomorrow,* 1948), probably Tuscaloosa, c. 1920

14. Octavus Roy Cohen, "The Fatted Half" (*Saturday Evening Post,* 1937), Birmingham, c. 1925

15. Sara Haardt, "Little White Girl" (*Scribner's Magazine,* 1934), plantation near Montgomery, c. 1925

16. F. Scott Fitzgerald, "Family in the Wind" (*Saturday Evening Post,* 1932), "Bending," Chilton County, 1932

17. Robert Gibbons, "Time's End" (*Atlantic Monthly,* 1942), probably Tuscaloosa County, c. 1933

18. Cecil Dawkins, "The Mourner" (*Paris Review,* 1961), "Galleton" [Birmingham], c. 1940

19. Eugene Walter, "I Love You Batty Sisters" (*Botteghe Oscure,* 1956), primarily Mobile, c. 1880-1940
20. Truman Capote, "My Side of the Matter" (*Tree of Night and Other Stories,* 1949), "Admiral's Mill," near Phenix City, c. 1945

The first interesting observation to be drawn from this grouping of twenty stories is that the order—chronological according to the action of each—suggests varied aspects of the history of the state. In "The Ginseng Gatherers" Daniel Glaze, who comes from a well-to-do, cultured family of Charleston, South Carolina, is living with his second wife on a vast tract of land on Little River; he gathers ginseng roots to sell in the capital at Tuscaloosa. Perhaps he can even find a "Chinaman" who will pay him pound for pound for the medicinal root highly prized in the Orient. "But failing Tuscaloosa, there was Mobile. He could stop at Demopolis on the way down. And he could find out about Montevallo and Huntsville." Daniel's first wife was a Cherokee Indian whom he married about 1829 when he first came to the headwaters of the Warrior. From her he has learned the Indian secrets of how to cook and dry fish and fruit, how to farm without toiling as his Bible-reading neighbors do—dogs and birds can be trained to do large portions of the work—and how to venerate the metaphysical spirits of rivers, springs, and coves. In short, in addition to serving in the state legislature as a spokesman for the Indians, Daniel has come to know the deep meaning of joy of the Indian way of life as he "strollops" through his green-thicket world.

Hooper's Simon Suggs, who "found himself as poor at the conclusion of the Creek war, as he had been at its commencement," attends a camp-meeting twenty miles from his native Tallapoosa and makes off with the collection funds that are supposed to be used to build a new church, since Mrs. Suggs had already warned him that "the sugar and coffee was nigh about out." Simon, son of a "hard-shell" Baptist preacher in Georgia, knows his church folk well: he can outjerk, outpray, and outjump anybody in an East Alabama camp-meeting just as handily as he could subsist off the contibutions intended for "Fort Suggs" during the late Indian war.

Also during these flush times in the old "South-West" Baldwin's Samuel Hele was earning a rare reputation in western Alabama as a lawyer of sharp and glib tongue. Squire Sam is persuaded to describe the region in such frightening terms that the unattractive New England school teacher, Miss Charity Woodey, will leave of her own accord. This

> new importation from Yankeedom—not from its factory of calicoes, but from its factory of school teachers . . . had been sent to order, from one of the interior villages of Connecticut. The Southern propensity of getting everything from abroad, had extended to school-mistresses,—though the country had any number of excellent and qualified girls wishing such employment at home . . . . *Dooty,* as she called it, was a great word with her. Conscience was another . . . . She had come out as missionary of light to the children of the South, who dwell in the darkness of Heathenesse.

Such a terrifying account does Sam give of this part of the state—its drunkenness, stealing, and race bigotry—that Miss Charity makes a hasty exit on the next morning's mail-stage, "ticketed on the Northern line."

> In the hurry of departure, a letter, addressed to Mrs. Harriet S____ was found, containing some interesting memoranda and statistics on the subject of slavery and its practical workings, which I should never have thought of again had I not seen something like them in a very popular fiction, or rather book of fictions, in which the slaveholders are handled with something less than feminine delicacy and something more than masculine unfairness.

Bierce's "An Occurrence at Owl Creek Bridge" and Peck's "Pap's Mules" are Civil War stories; the former takes place "in nothern Alabama," the latter in and around Oakville, Peck's name for Tuscaloosa. Both concern Confederate civilians and Yankee soldiers, and both depict the kind of individual combat, small skirmishes, raiding and burning that characterized the fighting in a state that was the scene of no major battle except that of Mobile Bay at the end of the war. In Bierce's story Peyton Farquhar, a young, well-to-do planter, is tricked by a disguised Federal scout into attempting sabotage of a railroad bridge thirty miles away at Owl Creek. For this he is hanged. But before he dies he imagines in a series of flashing glimpses that he escapes through the streams and woods he knows so well; he even reaches his own gate and "passes up the wide white walk."

"Pap's Mules" concerns the bravery of the Cline children, who half in innocence and half in derring-do, hide their father's mules from the raiding Yankees. Oakville falls to the raiders, but only after the city fathers shoot off their rusty old cannon. At the end of the story word comes that Lee has surrendered, and Mrs. Cline can again go about her housework "a-singin' Coronation":

Bring forth ther raw-yell di-er-dem
And cra-own Him Lor-or-ord of all.

In "The Mustydines Was Ripe" the Civil War years are over, and Benny Freeland is recalling his long walk from Georgia to Toadvine, just north of Birmingham, which was then "a wide place in the road—just six years old" but able to furnish a good beef stew, a saloon, and a marriage license from Judge Mudd's court. The joys of earth—the good clean spring water, the green forests, and self-sustaining farm of his father-in-law—these are the things Benny remembers as best after his love for Patsy, who has now been his wife for fifty years.

The stories of the twentieth century reflect more social than political history. In "Prelude" Selina Jo lives with her parents in a "two-room cabin of the saddle-bag type" on "a sandy land homestead—twenty-five miles from the nearest railroad—in that section of the country which borders the Gulf of Mexico." Because she longs for a gingham dress, she does manual labor in Pruitt's turpentine orchard. Finally, in order to escape from the influence of her poor white-trash family community, she makes her own way to the girls' reformatory in the county seat; Selina Jo wants to be reformed, "to be made different" from all her no-account Hudsill relatives.

"Whistles" is also set in south Alabama in the lumbering region of the state, where William March has created Hodgetown, the scene of several of his stories and novels. Mr. Ridley, now living in New York, has just seen a Broadway play that makes use of screaming whistles, and he remembers Hodgetown. He thinks of its mill whistles that controlled the lives of men and women—the men who ran the planer mills and the women like Mrs. Foley who operated the company boarding-house. Mr. Ridley now considers her one of the fortunate people of this world because she had known what her work was and did it vigorously. In ugly little Hodgetown with its "yellow frame houses . . . company office, and the sawmill itself, with men hurrying home from work, their shoulders covered with sawdust," Mrs. Foley had always felt that it was up to her "to wake up the world and wash its face, and feed it, and get it to work on time" after the whistles had blown.

The story " 'Lijah" addresses itself to an economic problem of the New South: a replacement for one-crop cotton farming. Judge Holmsted, the master of Holmacres, is about to lose his plantation. By a curious chain of events he entertains angels unaware in the persons of two Northerners who offer him $50,000 for his hill forty and its mica deposit. The Judge begins to see his dreams fulfilled: "broad fields fenced to pasture and dotted with sleek cattle and fat swine; bottom lands, yellow with ripening corn; Holmacres, with its doors once more flung wide . . . ."

"History of the South" deals with the same problems

applied to the social rather than to the agricultural scene. Annie Laurie Bourne Durville, daughter-in-law of a former state governor, is now a pitiful, poverty-stricken old woman. She has refused to marry "Northern" money, like her friends the Stillson sisters in Camden, or Southerners whose grandfathers were "in trade," as is the case of the narrator of the story. Just before she dies at eighty-eight she sends the walnut-framed portraits of her ancestors—"bishops, under the Stuarts, royal proprietors, governors of states . . ."—to the narrator, whose husband has now bought and restored Rosedale, Mrs. Durville's girlhood home. "She sent them to me," remarks the narrator, touched by this gift from one who has spent all her life talking about the Bournes, the Durvilles, the deGraffenrieds, and Pettuses. "Not to you . . . but to Rosedale," replies her husband.

In "Jericho, Jericho, Jericho" the theme is also that of the passing of the plantation way of life, as Kate McCowan lies dying in her eighty-seventh year. She remembers, as she waits for a last visit from her grandson, how she has struggled to maintain and sustain the four hundred acres of Long Gourd. She had wanted her grandson to marry a neighboring Carlisle girl because her inheritance "would give me a landing on the river." When Dick reveals that he plans to marry Eva Callahan, Mammy asks him where the girl comes from. " 'Birmingham,' she heard herself say with contempt. They could have lived there all their lives and still come from somewhere. I've got a mule older'n Birmingham." The climax comes when Mammy explains certain routine winter chores to Dick, who replies, "Eva will want to spend the winters in town." Mammy knows in that moment that all her land grabbing and monumental hard work have been for naught; Long Gourd is doomed.

In addition to discovering new ways of life after the Civil War and Reconstruction, Alabamians were naturally concerned with the perennial problems of personal relationships. "Departure of Hubbard" is a story about one such relationship; it is a wonderfully evocative remembrance of the meaning of boyhood in a small town, when towns were small enough for boys to encompass and make them their own. "In my country of boyhood [says the narrator] the house was called Home, the town was called Town, and the creek was called Yellow Creek." Hubbard swims in the nude with the gang in Yellow Creek, but he allows little Tommie to beat him dressing so that Tommie won't be last and called an "old squirming maggit." On the way home he promises his girl, Snookie Jamieson, that he'll wear a bathing suit and take her swimming tomorrow at Crawford's Lake. Hubbard has departed "into the borderland of youth."

The post-Civil War period in Alabama saw the emergence of Birmingham as the industrial complex of the state. With its rapid growth, a large Negro population flowed from the plantations and smaller farms into the city. "The Fatted Half" is a comic story of Florian Slappey's difficulties and final success in printing a "cullud social register" for the city and at the same time in keeping out the name of his financial backer's rival, Steve Bangs, who works in the Ensley steel mills. Despite the fact that the story treats the Negro as vaudeville comic, there are valid comments on social mores and memorable descriptions of Birmingham's all-Negro communities.

After Florian is met by a grand reception at the Terminal Station welcoming him home from Harlem to the tune of Professor Aleck Champagne's Jazzphony Orchestra, he "leaned back and drank in the warm April air of his beloved Birmingham. He gazed rapturously at the flowered crest of Red Mountain and eyed with approval the towering bulk of the big hotels and office buildings." As they rolled through the civic center of Birmingham's "Darktown,"

> Florian's nostrils were pleasantly assailed by the almost forgotten odor of genuine Birmingham barbecue .... His eyes rested contentedly upon the four-square architecture of the Penny Prudential Bank Building and he gave rapt attention to the blare of music from in front of the Champion and Frolic Theatres.

Jasper drove him on to Sis Callie Fluker's boarding-house, where he occupied the second floor front, looking down on the traffic of Avenue F on the edge of Tittisville, "fashionable cullud suburb." "Little White Girl" is a counterpart to both "The Fatted Half" and "Departure of Hubbard." It concerns the coming of age of Suzie Tarleton, who lives on a somewhat lonely plantation near Montgomery, totally unaware of race distinction; her maturing comes about when a new little white girl, Alicia, moves into a neighboring though distant plantation. Susie enjoys above all playing under "the big oak tree with its mauve cool shade" wonderful games with Pinky, a plantation Negro of her own age. When Susie tries to introduce Pinky to Alicia, the latter replies, "She's a nigger! . . . . You're entirely too big to play with her now." Pinky's mother, Aunt Hester, confirms this attitude as she explains to Pinky: "You kin go an' speak to [Susie] if it'll ease yo' pain but tell her you know the difference between a white chile and a black chile, an' y'all cain't play together no more. Hit wuz boun' to come. Quit that snufflin' an' go yonder an' tell her lak I told you."

"Family in the Wind" is a memorable account of the long-remembered spring tornadoes in Alabama during the bleak depression year of 1932. Samuel Minturn Peck, the state poet laureate living in Tuscaloosa, called the tornado that roared up the Warrior River Valley "the Wind of Death"; and Scott Fitzgerald, living in Montgomery at the time, called it, " . . . not a collection of sounds, it was just Sound itself; a great screeching bow drawn across the chords of the universe." This frightening natural phenomenon struck the countryside twice around Bending—Fitzgerald's fictional village in Chilton County—when people were already distressed and out of work. In the Janney family the eldest son Pinky lies unconscious with a bullet near the brain as a result of a recent "row in Birmingham." His farmer father is at odds with his own "educated" doctor-brother, who as a chronic alcoholic has returned recently to Bending, where the hospital has been closed for lack of patients. With their house completely demolished and their possessions scattered to the winds, the Janney family, like their neighbors, set about rebuilding. The storm having ruined his car, the "doc" leaves on a train for Montgomery to persuade the Red Cross to allow him to make a home for little Helen Kilrain, orphaned by the tragic loss of her people. And perhaps he can also find a new life for himself.

"Time's End" is a story of the continuing agricultural problem of growing cotton and managing the Negroes on the land. John Lipscomb's father has decided to give up growing it in the rich bottoms, where "the river gets one crop in three," and has moved all the Negroes up to Granmere, "just on the edge of town." It becomes John's unhappy job to persuade the ancient Mub and her daughter Glow to give up their cabin for new quarters. Though he succeeds in getting them to promise to move, when the van comes, Mub refuses: she is too old and her roots are too deep in " 'his low-life swamp." It was "like the end of a time . . . . Seeing Mub there, seeing her sitting there in her short-legged, hide-bottomed chair, seeing the voluminous checkered gingham about her little body, seeing her wrinkled and now ageless face, I was struck with the unchangingness of her."

"The Mourner," set in Galleton (Miss Dawkins' name for Birmingham), is concerned with the homecoming of Gabriel Orghesi to attend the funeral of his grandfather, an immigrant steel worker. Like Florian Slappey he arrives at the Terminal Station, "bright after the tunnell and the train. The people, the booths, the benches like pews in a church were small under the domed ceiling three or four lost stories high." Outside and alone, Gabriel looks down "the long avenue pointed toward the heart of the city. Across the mouth of the viaduct that spanned the railroad yard, the neon sign bubbled—GALLETON, THE MAGIC CITY . . . . Atop Bald Mountain the Iron Man held his torch." Gabriel takes a cab across town past the fairgrounds and "the motel like an Indian village" to his home on a hill in Ensley. There he sees again his priest-brother, his *mama mia,* and all the confining "Southern-Italian-Catholic background" that drove him to seek his artistic career in California. After the funeral full of memories, his return on the train cannot come too soon, escaping his possessive mother in the charade of her pretending to go West with him.

The last two stories in this proposed collection are somewhat comic treatments of what has come to be called the Southern Gothic grotesque. "I Love You Batty Sisters" concerns Belladair, aged eighty, and Mary Cross, aged eighty-two, who have played a strange game all their lives of never going back to places they have enjoyed. Montgomery, for example, has been ruled out because they had such a marvelous time at the opening of the Jesse French Piano Company when, dressed in their Gainesborough hats, they banged out *I Want My Chicken Back* for all the guests of the store. Birmingham, Atlanta, New Orleans are also soon ruled out, and even their native Mobile must be struck because they enjoyed too much the ride downtown in the black maria with a burglar who broke into their house. But finally their world becomes too small, so they decide to start over. In their eighties they venture out again to shop for "some good okra." They have determined to rediscover the world instead of merely nursing their "forty-year-old Boston fern that was descended from one belonging to Augusta Evans Wilson, the celebrated author of *St. Elmo.*"

In "My Side of the Matter" there are also two weirdly warped sisters, Eunice and Olivia-Ann, who enjoy dominating their niece Margie and trying to separate her from her sixteen-year-old husband, who has given up his "perfectly swell position clerking at the Cash 'n' Carry" in Mobile. These unhealthy events take place in a big yellow house with "real columns" and a yard lined with red and white japonicas. The geographical setting is Admiral's Mill ("pop.

342") somewhere between Eufaula *[sic]* and Phoenix *[sic]* City, "a damn gap in the road any way you care to consider it," according to the disgruntled husband narrating his side of the matter.

In these brief digests of twenty stories ordered by the chronology of their events, some of the historical and sociological patterns of the development of the state are evident. Telling judgments are made about the land and its people from the Indian days and the first white settlers through the wild frontier times, the establishment of large plantations, the Civil War and Reconstruction, ensuing social upheaval, and the emergence of cities against a background of racial unrest and agricultural readjustment and depression. It can, of course, be argued that writers of fiction often consult works of history in the process of their own writing and thus create a kind of pseudo, secondhand history. With mediocre historical fiction this may sometimes be the case, but one of the by-products of all good fiction is that it re-creates history in the patterns of people living and struggling—not merely being born, voting, going to war, and dying in an objective vacuum of names, dates, causes, and effects. Fiction is history as the average man knows it and lives it in his own fragmented world.

It is further evident that this limited sample of short fiction depicts the main regions of the state. Here are glimpses into Mobile, Baldwin County, Lockhart and the Piney Woods along with the Black Belt plantations in the south; the Tennessee Valley, the headwaters of the Warrior River, and Birmingham in the north; "Wynnesborough" on the Tombigbee, Tuscaloosa, and Gainesville in the west; and Chilton County, Tallapoosa, and "Admiral's Mill" in the Piedmont and the southeast. The various regions of a geographically diversified state are well represented.

The second observation to be made from this grouping of twenty stories concerns the authors. In selecting these stories little attention was paid to whether a writer was an Alabamian or not. The criterion was always how well does he write about Alabama. All except four, however, were actually born in Alabama or spent significant portions of their lives in the state. The exceptions—Bierce, Fitzgerald, Lytle, and Capote—are writers of national and international reputations.

Ambrose Bierce was familiar with Alabama as a Federal soldier during the Civil War. His Ninth Indiana Regiment fought over much of the Deep South, and went into winter quarters at Huntsville in 1864-65. After his discharge Bierce became an agency aide for the Treasury Department in Selma, a town which he describes as "little better than a ruin; in the concluding period of the war General Wilson's cavalry had raided it and nearly destroyed it." There is little doubt that Bierce's reminiscences about Selma and the state as a whole during the sad post-war days are among the most interesting on record. Portions of his *Bits of Biography,* particularly "Way down in Alabam'," and "Four Days in Dixie," are composed of numerous miniature short stories. One of the most exciting is an account of transporting six hundred bales of Government cotton down the Tombigbee to Mobile. It is probably the best narrative about Alabama in the early days of Reconstruction.

The last sentence of the incident, along with much similar material elsewhere, indicates that Bierce's sympathy lay with a people in a beaten land suffering under unrealistic, harsh regulations. When the Government ship is waylaid by former Confederates who believed the cotton did not belong to the United States, the guarding Federal soldiers suddenly discover that they have no ammunition. Shots are fired only by Treasury agent Bierce and a Confederate "guest," who has been given a ride to Mobile. After the ship has luckily drifted out of the bandits' range, Bierce inquires about the firing that perhaps saved him from hanging (the fate of his predecessor in Selma). The last sentence of the narrative reads: "I allowed it was mouty cleaver in you-all to take me on, seein' I hadn't ary cent, so I thought I'd just kinder work my passage."

Just as the Civil War brought Bierce to Alabama, World War I brought Minnesotan F. Scott Fitzgerald to Camp Sheridan near Montgomery, and in 1920 he married Zelda, daughter of Judge and Mrs. Anthony Dickinson Sayre. After his demobilization Fitzgerald made many trips to Montgomery trying to persuade Zelda to marry him, at least twice after their marriage they seriously considered "permanently" living there, and all during his married life—especially during his wife's mental breakdowns and periods of convalescence— he spent protracted stays there, commenting once: "I like it. We have a nice house and a fine Stutz car (cost $400) and I'm going to do lots of work." From time to time Fitzgerald made use of his knowledge of Alabama in his fiction: he found it "a languid paradise of dreamy skies and firefly evenings and noisy niggery street fairs—and especially of gracious, soft-voiced girls, who were brought up on memories instead of money." His fictional name for the Montgomery he and Zelda had known—its side streets, cemeteries, swimming pools, clubs, gardens, taxis, and hotels—is sometimes "Tarleton in southern-most Georgia" and sometimes "a city in southern Tennessee." In "The Ice Palace," "The Last of the Belles," "The Sensible Thing," and "I Didn't Get Over" Fitzgerald uses Alabama background to advantage. And in "Family in the Wind" he writes one of his best stories of what Arthur Mizener calls "transmuted biography"—Zelda's schizophrenia is the tornado, he is alcoholic Doc Janney, and little Helen who hugs close her cat is his own daughter Scottie. During the last year of his life he wrote Scottie, then a student at Vassar but visiting her mother in Montgomery: "Maybe you can write something down there. It is a grotesquely pictorial country as I found out long ago and as Mr. Faulkner has since abundantly demonstrated."

Andrew Lytle, though born in Tennessee, has spent extended periods of his life on his father's farm near Guntersville, Alabama; he knows the Tennessee Valley at first hand, as the reader is aware from the skillful use of local detail in "Jericho, Jericho, Jericho." Truman Capote, though born in New Orleans, also knows Alabama from his many visits to the state. "My Side of the Matter" is not his only use of the Alabama countryside. *The Grass Harp* is set somewhere between Mobile and Brewton, both of which are mentioned in the novel.

It can be said with accuracy, then, that all of these sixteen writers have known Alabama at first hand. Like Sara Haardt, who married H.L. Mencken and lived the latter part of her life in Baltimore, many have lived or do now live in other parts of the country; but all have spent periods of their lives in the state and have written more than one story about its land and people.

Four of the authors are represented by two stories, not because of a lack of material to choose from but because they are writers of distinction whose fiction, long and short, consistently employs an Alabama setting. Many others might have been included had space permitted. In 1903 Tennesseean John Trotwood Moore was planning "Songs and Stories of Alabama," a work that was never published, though he did complete a number of "Black Belt stories" like "A Possum Hunt in Alabama" and "Runaway Rip." One of his best Alabama stories is "Tom's Last Forage" (1897), based on an incident in the life of his father, Judge John Moore of Marion. Louise-Clarke Prynelle's *Diddie, Dumps, and Tot or Plantation Child-Life* (1882), with its episodic construction like that of *Simon Suggs* and *Flush Times* is dedicated to her "dear Father, Dr. Richard Clarke, of Selma, Alabama"; Ruby Pickens Tartt continues the spirit of these recollections in her "Alabama Sketches" in the *Southwest Review* of 1944. Wyatt Blasingame's distinguished story "Man's Courage" deals with race relations in the army; William Cobb's "The Stone Soldier" concerns a post-Civil War monument salesman; Julian Lee Rayford has written a number of interesting tales and legends of the Alabama Gulf coast area; and

Welbourn Kelley, Lella Warren, Hampton S. Smith, Jr., Donald Wetzel, and Shirley Ann Grau have all reflected the Alabama scene. A number of writers who in their formative years studied with Hudson Strode at the University of Alabama might well be represented here in addition to Gibbons and Hassell, but *Spring Harvest* (1944) records their promising work. Two examples subsequent to 1944 are Borden Deal's "Exodus," an excellent story of the displacement of people by the mechanical cotton picker, set somewhere near the Alabama-Mississippi border, and John Craig Stewart's "The Last Day," depicting the grim life and death of a foreman in a cotton mill.

Despite this wealth of material William March, Howell Vines, Edgar Valentine Smith, and Robert Gibbons are here represented by two stories because they have written much long and short fiction about Alabama, and their work deserves the kind of sampling that more than one story permits. Any anthology is always slightly better if it can be selective in depth as well as in breadth.

Regardless of the distinction of its authors, however, even an imaginary anthology should be dependent more upon the quality of its individual selections than upon any ingenuity of its arrangement. The stories in "Alabama in the Short Story" may be appealing to those who have an interest in the state, but the quality of the volume as a whole would depend upon the quality of the fiction apart from its setting and themes. Unfortunately this quality in short fiction is not easy to define and frequently not easy to defend. Fashions in writing like other fashions change, and when the selections are spread over more than a century, a true judgment of quality is often lost in a judgment of superficial timeliness.

The stories of Hooper and Baldwin are representative of the humorous tales based largely on exaggeration—a tradition that culminated in the work of Mark Twain. The exaggeration of Sam Hele's account to Miss Woodey about local conditions is a masterpiece of high comedy. When Miss Woodey asks if there is much stealing in the neighborhood, Sam replies, "All they got they got, directly or indirectly, in that way . . . . Madam, if New-York, Mobile, and New Orleans were to get their own, they might enclose the whole town, and label the walls the lost and stolen office." In addition to such amusing overstatement these tales often provide touches of realism that predict later tendencies in fiction. When Mrs. Suggs is trying to push Simon into action, she reminds him that there is "not a dozen j'ints and middlins *all put together,* in the smokehouse."

The last two stories, written over a hundred years later, are somewhat like these first two. Though the plot is subordinated, the character of the narrator takes on a new dominance instead of the usual omniscient third person; and the acquiring of this narrator's point of view instead of a search for "what finally happens" becomes the impelling motif. Both stories are broadly humorous in their exaggeration of the grotesque, and both make a special point of much realistic detail to subdue the weird into the partially believable. The young husband in "My Side of the Matter," who is forced to sleep on the unscreened back porch, describes the varmints in this swampy part of the state: " . . . mosquitoes that could murder a buffalo, given half a chance, not to mention dangerous flying roaches and a posse of local rats big enough to haul a wagon train . . . ." In technique both these stories refine character and especially point of view. As narratives they seem more sophisticated, but they do not tell such exciting events as their century-old predecessors.

The stories of Peck, Bierce, and Smith represent a type of fiction that was refined through the latter part of the nineteenth and early twentieth centuries; it is sometimes called the well-made story. In character, plot, setting, and idea it strives for a judicious blend; there is a beginning, a middle, and a resolution. Nothing is left in an equivocal state as it often is in the on-goingness of actual life: Peyton Farquhar's body is hanged though his spirit escapes to the love of home and the countryside of heart's desire; Pap's mules are saved and the war ends; Selina Jo gets her wish to be reformed; and Judge Holmsted saves his plantation.

But with writers like March, Fitzgerald, Lytle, Haardt, Dawkins, and Gibbons a new type of story is evident—one that has dominated the writing of fiction for the past forty years. A situation rather than a plot emerges, and the real artistry of the story lies in the reader's becoming aware of the situation from the many indirections that actual existence often seems to pursue. A drummer realizes that all his glib talk will not keep the fact of death from his family; a tornado makes an alcoholic doctor realize that an old life needs to be violently blown away; a grandmother perceives that her plantation will not endure after her death; a child learns that she can no longer have black and white playmates; a boy becomes aware that his brother is growing up; and an artist perceives why he must remain apart from the repressive background of his Italian-Catholic youth in the Alabama melting pot of Birmingham.

Occasionally writers develop an approach to the short story that is somewhat unusual. Howell Vines, for example, builds his fiction around setting as a reality—symbolic as well as physical in force—in the same way that Elizabeth Bowen has made atmosphere forceful in her many British stories. His ginseng roots and "mustydines" foreshadow the decisions of his characters in addition to symbolizing the mysteries of the Orient-Indian world and the healthy sanity of ripe young love. Daniel Glaze seeks the root prized in the Orient just as he has sought to understand the Jefferson County countryside from the perspective of the psychic wisdom of the Indians; Benny feels that he must marry Patsy on Sunday, and fifty years have proved the rightness and ripeness of his decision. By cultivating a purposefully flat, unobtrusive style, Vines succeeds in impressing his readers with the significance of dusty roads, green fields, thick woods, clear springs, and bright rivers and canebreaks of an earlier world.

The technique of Hassell and Walter is also distinctive. They intimate a broad expanse of time and place—material enough for a novel. But by a careful control of theme—a device brought to an artistic high-point in the stories of Katherine Anne Porter—both Hassell and Walter confine themselves to the limits of the short story. Hassell explores only the problem of money and Southern aristocracy, while Walter is concerned only with withdrawal and emergence into the daily world.

Somewhat different from the other stories in this listing is the work of Octavus Roy Cohen. Too often popular fiction is omitted from any consideration because of its slick surface, trite style, and type characters. All of these faults Cohen has, but at least the sheer bulk of his more than 250 stories about "Darktown Birmingham" entitles him to some recognition. The slickness of his surfaces, as well as the ingenuity of his ideas, is intimated by the outrageous puns of some of his titles like "Noblesse Obliged," "Night Blooming Serious," "Oft in the Silly Night," "Lilies of the Alley," "Ham and Exit," "Low but Sure," and "Black to Nature."

To demonstrate in detail the quality of these twenty stories would exceed the scope of this essay, since such a process would require individual analyses of each. It should be noted, however, that most of them made their first appearances in the better magazines and quarterlies of the last fifty years: *Harper's Magazine, Atlantic Monthly, Southern Review, Story, Scribner's Magazine, Midland, Botteghe Oscure,* and *Paris Review.* The more popular magazines like *Good Housekeeping, Saturday Evening Post,* and *Woman's Home Companion* are also represented. Another superficial indication of quality is the fact that almost all of the twentieth-century authors have made appearances in the annual edition of *The Best American Short Stories* and *The O. Henry Prize Stories.*

These Alabama stories of the past one hundred years depict not only the history, land, and people of the state; they also underscore the chief trends of American short fiction from the tall tale of the old Southwest, to the well-integrated stories of the end of the nineteenth century, to the diversified fiction of the last forty years with its Jamesian weavings and comments on character and idea. From Simon Suggs and Sam Hele to Batty Sisters and "The Mourner" is a long and entertaining road.

4

Samuel Minturn Peck, Gentleman of Letters

THE Alabama Legislature created the State Laureateship in 1931 to honor Samuel Minturn Peck for his long poetic career and to compensate for a conspicuous absence of poets either native or adopted. Before Peck's day, A.B. Meek and William Russell Smith had written imitative and enthusiastic verses, and Father Ryan had spent a decade in Mobile after the banner of the Confederacy had been furled. But there has been no Edgar Allan Poe, no Henry Timrod, no Sidney Lanier, no William Alexander Percy, no Allen Tate, or John Crowe Ransom. Even though Peck cannot be compared with the best poets of surrounding Southern states, he occupies a unique place in the literature of Alabama, for he is one of the few professional men of letters who, born in the state, continued to live and work within its bounds. Peck devoted to creative writing some fifty years unencumbered with other professional duties. During these years he produced articles and travelogues for newspapers such as the New Orleans *Times-Democrat* and numerous "sketches" for magazines such as *Collier's Weekly* and *Leslie's Weekly.* After he collected in 1902 eleven of these in *Alabama Sketches,* Peck turned his energies with little success to the writing of novels. He believed that first and last and always he was a "singer."

Between 1886 and 1925 Peck published seven volumes of verse: *Cap and Bells* (1886), *Rings and Love Knots* (1892),

Rhymes and Roses (1895), *Fair Women of To-day* (1895), *The Golf Girl* (1899), *Maybloom and Myrtle* (1910), and *The Autumn Trail* (1925). The readers of the Boston *Evening Transcript* noted his contributions for a period of some thirty years, countless grade-school scholars of the late nineteenth and early twentieth centuries have recited "The Grapevine Swing," "A Knot of Blue" was once popular with "the boys at Yale," and countless parlor sopranos sang musical settings for his ballades, rondeaux, villanelles, and triolets.

In 1926 Wightman F. Melton reported in the Atlanta *Georgian* that "The Grapevine Swing" was perhaps the best-known poem in American literature, that its refrain was far more familiar to students at the University of Georgia than the most often quoted passages of Poe, Longfellow, or Whitman. And even more surprising, Melton asserted, it proved to be the only poem that the students themselves could quote to any extent. This familiarity attested not only the widespread use of the poem in grade-school readers but also the broad appeal of its sentimental nostalgia:

> When I was a boy on the old plantation,
>   Down by the deep bayou,
> The fairest spot of all creation,
>   Under the arching blue;
> When the wind came over the cotton and corn,
>   To the long slim loop I'd spring
> With brown feet bare and a hat-brim torn,
>   And swing in the grapevine swing.
> Swinging in the grapevine swing,
> Laughing where the wild birds sing,
>   I dream and sigh
>   For the days gone by
> Swinging in the grapevine swing . . . .

About the time of the Georgia "familiar poem" test, Donald Davidson—Vanderbilt professor, poet, and critic—wrote Peck an answer to the latter's complaint about obscurity in the poems of *The Fugitive,* expressing pleasure at being noticed by

one whose place high on the Southern Parnassus is known to everybody. I learned "The Grapevine Swing" when I was a boy,— having heard it many a time from my father's lips,—and it is one of the poems marked immortal in my memory.

When Peck was asked to read before the Alabama Writers' Conclave in 1930, one of the two poems he selected was "The Grapevine Swing," which he had published in 1892. When he changed publishers from Frederick Stokes to Dana Estes in 1910, there appeared on the flyleaf of *Maybloom and Myrtle,* "By Samuel Minturn Peck/Author of 'The Grapevine Swing.' " The poem appeared in numerous anthologies, and it was almost never omitted from collections of Southern poetry compiled between 1890 and 1920. In short, when Peck is remembered at all, it is as a one-poem poet. Nothing else he ever wrote achieved the popularity of "The Grapevine Swing."

Peck was a static poet. From the 1886 volume, *Cap and Bells,* through the 1925 volume, *The Autumn Trail,* he did not alter the easy flow of the versification, the triteness of intellectual and emotional appeal, and the preference for the general rather than the specific image. In 1886 Peck wrote of Alabama:

Know'st thou that balmy Southern land,
By myrtles crowned, by zephyrs fanned,
Where verdant hills and forests grand
    Smile 'neath an azure dome?

And in 1925, although the diction has become less "poetic," the same rhythmical generalities abound:

Daisy-land, O Daisy-land!
    A child, I wandered there;

Now is it yet a hazy land,
To memory ever fair.
It is so blue, so blue above—
I see no more such skies.
Its blossoms seem to breathe of love,
And dew from paradise.

A large number of Peck's poems in all the volumes concern lovely women. In *Cap and Bells* there is "Dollie":

She displays a tiny glove,
And a dainty little love
Of a shoe;
And she wears her hat a-tilt
Over bangs that never wilt
In the dew.

And in 1910 *Maybloom and Myrtle* furnishes illustrations of the same sentiments in the same verse form:

I know a little maid
May her beauty never fade!
And her fan,
May its flutter never cease:
Though it robbed my heart of peace
In Japan.

In 1892 the reviewer in the *Critic* called attention to this lack of development in Peck's verse. After commenting upon their smooth rhythm and technical finish, he says: "We cannot see that he [Peck] had anywise advanced his art, or attempted any more serious flights of song." As a matter of fact, Peck's last listed work in the *Reader's Guide* of 1933 is the poem "Autumn Glee" of 1892 with only the title changed to " 'Tis All a Myth that Autumn Grieves."

The same retrospection upon an unreal, ideal past is evident in Peck's letters and in those of his literary friends. As he deplores the influence of Whitman, so he dislikes Amy Lowell, Ezra Pound, and Harriet Monroe. In February, 1922,

Mrs. Julia W. Baker, columnist and newspaper poet of New Orleans with whom Peck long conducted a prolific correspondence, writes: "I agree with you about Harriet Monroe; inspiration is lacking in her verse, or even impulse." And in April of that year: "I am glad fat Amy is being snubbed in England. Have you noticed that there are several yawps by Sandburg in the current Century?" Along with his dislike for these poets, Peck also disapproved of the verse experiments of his fellow Alabamian, Clement Wood, author of "Shortnin' Bread," and what he considered blatant coteries of self-advertisement. In a satiric holograph poem, "The Poet and the Pixie," Peck holds imaginary conversation with a fairy of literary insight:

In fairy land we often chat of authors when we meet,
Especially of those who in their qualities compete.
Sometimes I have been queried—I'd not answer if I could—
Which is the more retiring—William Benét or Clement Wood . . . .
"But literary game there is, of every kind a lot—
Indeed 'tis so abundant it seems waiting to be shot."
"Surely, Sir, there must be some good writers in your ken;
Forsooth, you would not shoot them all, the women and the men?"
"Be not alarmed," the Pixie smiled "nor look so very solemn— you—
Nor think that I've in mind today an authors' St. Bartholomew."

After the turn of the century Peck felt himself "somewhat passé," a Victorian, prim and orderly, after the manner of Praed, Dobson, and Locker-Lampson. Peck's friend, the distinguished Columbia professor, scholar, and poet, George E. Woodberry, who shared his disapproval of the modern world, summarizes their feeling in a letter of March, 1926:

I am glad to see you still thrum the lyre, at least—but in the 'large discourse' of the most modern bards there is little hope for us of the last age, I fear.—Success to your songs, nevertheless, I cry,—and many a good wish for your comfort and happiness.

The spirit of looking backward increased with age, and it became a sort of fad with Peck to think of himself as the sweet singer of the idyllic South. In 1932 Hoyt Hudson remarked of him: "You cannot please him better, nor pay him a more sincere compliment, than by calling him old-fashioned."

There is yet another striking aspect of Peck's poetic career: he was a faithful devotee of newspaper publication. Interviewed by a New York newspaper reporter in 1895, he lamented the lack of Southern publishing houses and literary journals. "The writers of the South depend very largely, Mr. Peck said, on their newspapers as a means of gaining a foothold." His own poetic debut was made with "The Orange Tree" in the New York *Evening Post* in 1878, when he was working for his M.D. at Bellevue. And in 1925 on the flyleaf of his last volume, *The Autumn Trail,* appears this note: "All the poems in this volume not credited to other publications have appeared from time to time in the Boston Transcript."

In between these two dates hundreds of Peck's poems appeared in newspapers. Editors frequently wrote to thank him for his contributions, and often they requested permission to reprint or asked for a new poem. The Boston *Evening Transcript,* New York *Sun* and *Tribune,* Philadelphia *Ledger,* Wilmington *Every Evening,* Atlanta *Journal,* Birmingham *News* and *Age-Herald,* New Orleans *Times-Democrat,* Arkansas *Gazette,* Nashville *Banner,* Louisville *Courier-Journal*—all published Peck's verse. The fact that for about thirty years the Boston *Evening Transcript* regularly printed Peck's verse is extraordinary. Sometimes his poems appeared monthly; again they would appear several times a week. His admirers wrote him letters, and E.F. Edgett, longtime editor and literary adviser to the *Transcript,* wrote him many notes thanking him for poems sent and assuring him of a ready welcome for future ones. These notes frequently reminded the author that as many reprints on slick paper were available as he desired. The reprints Peck kept and filed away, sometimes with marginal notations for future changes, a convenient method of obtaining a typesetting. Then too the readers of the *Transcript* were assured of sweet-flowing songs that would never shock their sensibilities. T.S. Eliot's "Cousin Harriet" would have approved of such of Mr. Peck's verses as "Shattered Roses" and "Garden Sonnets."

If the young Eliot ever chanced to read the verses of Samuel Minturn Peck in the *Transcript,* he would probably not have expressed his feeling so kindly as did William Rose Benét some years later in the *Saturday Review of Literature* when he remarked: "We like the author and his pleasant, simple lines, but we cannot find his work of great value." And if Samuel Minturn Peck ever chanced to read T.S. Eliot's "The Boston Evening Transcript," he very probably would have considered it another "yawp" by a modern poet who did not even have the dignity to sign himself Thomas Stearns Eliot.

Peck was too intelligent not to realize that his flair was really for newspaper verse. To his friend Julia Baker he even compared himself to Edgar Guest, for she writes him: "How can you compare yourself with that awful Edgar Guest? . . . . Edgar Pest . . . ." She assures him that his melodies are simple, true and inspired, like Tom Moore's. And this was surely what Peck wanted in his heart to believe. He wanted to ignore the fact that he made a fad of newspaper publication because only rarely did the "better" magazines accept his verse—he wanted to forget that his publishing ventures had of necessity been backed by his pocketbook. Only the first volume, *Cap and Bells,* went through five editions; the others sold less and less. From Frederick Stokes to Dana Estes to the Bookfellows and the Torch Press was not mere shifting of publishers; it was a literary descent. In reality, Peck was a journalistic poet who abhorred the word *journalism.* As late as 1915 he advised an aspiring young Arkansas poet, Jerry Williams, who had sent him *A Handful of Lyrics:* "A suggestion—why sign 'Jerry'? It savors of journalism and literary mortality. Be 'Jerry' to your comrades at a 'smoker,' but . . . ."

Another characteristic of Peck's work is its unevenness. Although a reader barely tolerates the pun in *vers de société* like

> And I'm as proud as any prince,
>   All honors I disdain;
> She says I am her rain beau since
>   I kissed her in the rain.

he nonetheless admits the homely sincerity of "My Grandmother's Turkey-Tail Fan":

> Though shorn of its glory, e'en now it exhales
>   An odor of hymn-books and snuff.
> Its primeval grace, if you like, you can trace:
>   'Twas limned for the future to scan,
> Just under a smiling gold-spectacled face,
>   My grandmother's turkey-tail fan.

Peck's vapid generality in "An Alabama Garden":

> Along a pine-clad hill it lies,
> O'erlooked by limpid Southern skies,
> A spot to feast a fairy's eyes,
>   A nook for happy fancies.

is in contrast to the precise images of "The Autumn Lane":

> A song for the autumn lane
>   O'erhung by sumacs and pines,
> Where the spider weaves a tremulous skein
>   In a mist of silvery lines;
>   And the asters gleam
>   By the wayside stream
> And peep through the yellowing vines;

And the wild mint's prayer
Floats quaint on the air
In the shade of the muscadines.

The banality of figure and the unfortunate rime in "A Twilight Picture" are obvious:

At the hour of twilight stilly
In a cozy window nook,
Softly bending like a lily
Breathless o'er a story-book
Sitteth Edith;
As she readeth
Pity shines in every look.

But beside his should be placed the fluency and sustained tone of "Foreboding":

If love could pass as die away
The summer winds at ebb of day
That through the amber silence stray,
Sweet heralds of repose,
Whispering in the ear of Night
The memory of the morning's light,
The fragrance of its rose,
Then we might live and never dread
The awful void when love is dead.

Like many another poet, Peck was unaware of the vast difference between his good and his poor work. In writing about his best poem in a letter to Mrs. Marie Bankhead Owen in 1930, he makes no mention of the only sonnet he ever published in a magazine of first rank—*Harper's:*

Communion

I send my love unto my dead each day;
Know not how; I only know it goes
Forth from my heart, and, going ever grows;
That as it flies, there's nothing can affray;

That, like a dove, it fondly keeps its way
Through dark and light along the path it knows;
That in its faithful flight it never slows,
And if I toil or sleep goes not astray.
I send my love unto my dead, and they—
They know 'tis sent, that I have not forgot;
For often when I am alone I feel
Their love return—and, oh, no words can say
The peace that comes to me! It matters not
What woes betide, I have wherewith to heal.

Instead of this sonnet Peck copies out what he evidently considers his best poem from *The Autumn Trail:*

Spectres

Not great ambitions gone astray
And lost forever by the way;
Not buds of youthful hope once bright
Grown withered in approaching night—
   Not these the phantoms of my heart
   That haunt me and will not depart.

Good deeds bethought but not begun,
The kindly acts so easy done;
Sad eyes I might have comforted;
The sorrows of the loved—and dead—
   These are the ghosts that bring me dole,
   And cast a shadow on my soul.

and adds this comment: "I never wrote a lyric more from my heart than this." While "Communion" is surely no great poem, it is a sonnet of sustained mood that approaches lyric fluency. Unfortunately Peck was insensitive to the differences between his rimed doggerel and his creditable lyrics.

As Peck was in his first volume, *Cap and Bells,* so is he in *The Autumn Trail;* the smart humor may have given way to a quiet seriousness, but the same preference for "poetic"

subjects, obvious rimes, and shallow sentiments still abounds.
He who wore the cap and bells goes

> Winding down the autumn trail
> [Finding] much that's fair to see;
> Fragrant odors scent the gale,
> Singing yet are bird and bee;
> Still the purple hills afar
> Lure me onward as I roam—
> But, alas, the evening star
> Soon will call the wanderer home.

After the 1932 spring tornado swept up the Black Warrior
Valley, Peck as the State Laureate commemorated the
tragedy when

> Bewildered memory strives in vain
> To hush the tortured cry
> Of mangled forms in dark and rain
> When the Wind of Death went by.

After the Legislature adopted a new State Seal, Peck wrote
suitable verses to be printed along with it in the *Alabama
Historical Quarterly*. He was an old hand at this game, for all
his life he had made verses to order.

His life too had been a long one: from the days prior to
the Civil War to the eve of World War II. Peck was born on
November 4, 1854, near Tuscaloosa. He attended the
University of Alabama, whose buildings had been destroyed
by Federal troops and whose resources were meager and
limited in the difficult days of Reconstruction. After he had
completed an M.D. at Bellevue Hospital Medical College to
satisfy his father, Peck studied languages and literature at
Columbia and later at the Alliance Français in Paris.

In his mature years Peck gave the impression of a Southern
gentleman of the genteel tradition. Accompanying the 1895

interview in a New York newspaper is a pen-and-ink sketch showing the author in a modish Panama hat and a sport coat, leisurely reading on a comfortable bench under one of the old oaks before his plantation cottage. In 1906 in the Nashville *Banner* Richard H. Yancey described him as a man "of simple build, tall and broad-shouldered, ruddy of complexion, and of a wholesome and genial temperament that makes and holds friends." As a rather attractive bachelor, well dressed in clothes from Rogers Peet and with a trust fund of some $100,000, Peck was a much sought-after dinner guest and a minor celebrity wherever he might be spending the season—whether it was Norwich, Connecticut; Hot Springs, Arkansas; or Boston and New York.

The career of Samuel Minturn Peck has a tragic negativeness about it—the negativeness of one who never quite made up his mind, preferring the inherent contradiction to the clear-cut decision. In his prose and verse he seems to see himself as the professional Southerner, the guardian of the traditions of the Old South. But his father's connection with the Radical administration as Chief Justice of the Alabama Supreme Court always made his Southern conscience rest uneasy. In his letters is frequent complaint about the circumscribing and deadening life in a little Southern town, yet Peck was never able to keep himself away from Tuscaloosa for any length of time. Mrs. Baker writes him from New Orleans: " . . . you should not bury yourself in Alabama. Whether you like it or not, you should flock with the literati. As you say, if you are not on the spot, and of the clique, you are ignored." And again: "I am glad you are going to leave Tuscaloosa, and go where you will find more intellectual stimulus." But he never did. It was Hot Springs, New York, Boston, London, Paris, Rome—then back to Tuscaloosa.

He was the M.D. who never practiced, and objected to being called Doctor. He rimed again and again about the charms and beauties of women, but never married. He had inherited a sufficient income to support himself all of his life without being concerned about earning a living. He had leisure, an agile mind, and a good ear. Yet with all, he was a dilettante: he experienced a popularity that came too early and too easily. His belated-Romantic ideas of prose and verse that were acceptable to American publishers and editors of the eighties and nineties were doomed. And these notions he rigidly refused to change. His views about versifying and his advice to the young poets of the post World War I generation are admirably summarized in the following manuscript poem:

Advice to Poets

If Waller, living, piped about
    A "lovely Rose" today,
He'd pipe in vain beyond a doubt,
    And throw his time away.
Keats' "thing of beauty's" out of date
    And "faery lands forlorn";
Nor would John Milton dare to prate
    Of "incense-breathing morn."

Ye bards who now to fame aspire
    Should slaughter sing, or slums,
Desert the lute and leave the lyre
    For trumpets or for drums;
Not maiden's sighs but dead men's eyes
    Upstaring from the trenches
Should be your theme, if ye are wise—
And don't forget your stenches.

Like Henry James, Peck often found his countrymen somewhat crude, but he could never become an expatriate. Like his friend George E. Woodberry he longed for the graces of times past and the imagined elegance of earlier days, but he always continued to strive for popular success.

Although Peck's prose fiction is less well known than his

poetry, in the light of the nationwide interest in regional local-color fiction that grew up after the Civil War, his short stories occupy an unusual place in the literary history of Alabama. Sometime during the 1890's Peck decided to have a try at prose fiction. Consciously or unconsciously he must have felt a desire to join what amounted to a Southern prose renascence in the closing years of the century, when such writers as Mary N. Murfree, John Trotwood Moore, Richard M. Johnson, Joel Chandler Harris, and Thomas Nelson Page were writing romantic "sketches" of Tennessee, Georgia, and Virginia. Peck was right in perceiving a ready market and a waiting audience. Raw materials were at hand and models for the sentimental local-color sketch abounded. Since the vogue of Bret Harte the country had been flooded with tales saturated with dialect and genteel realism. The short prose fiction of the period strained after the clever incident and coincidental circumstance. Thomas Bailey Aldrich was the high priest of originality, and O. Henry was shortly to push this type of story to its ultimate. Since Peck was no innovator and had little apparent interest in the problems of the art of fiction, he assumed the fashions of popular journalism of the nineties, often embodying some of its unfortunate characteristics. His very titles, for example, almost overreach themselves: "The Poet and the Pink Breakfast," "The Second Mrs. Battleboro's First Thanksgiving," and "How Willett Wooed the Widow."

In the closing years of the century Peck published about twenty-five stories in such magazines as *The Outlook, Leslie's Weekly* (with illustrations by Howard Chandler Christy), *The Independent* and *The Illustrated American.* The subject matter of these tales is generally of three types: romantic comedies of the drawing-room variety, neatly packaged items of the bizarre and the coincidental, and incidents of the Civil War and Reconstruction.

An example of the first type is "John Sedgwick's Valentine," a tale of rather obvious surprises. John Sedgwick of "Northport in West Alabama" receives a proposal of marriage from Charlotte Baker, whom he does not love. After being rebuffed by his true love, Nora Cummings, John accidentally addresses a "lineament cure" to her, when he is helping his drug-clerk friend, Tom Craig. The accident turns the scales, and Nora capitulates because she believes that John truly has her on his mind and heart.

An illustration of the second type is "The Dragon Candlestick." Dollie and her bereaved mother have sometime ago been left a strange Italian candlestick to be used only when the shadows of misfortune seem to be closing in upon them. These shadows of death and poverty have now come, and when the candles are lighted the hot wax melts open a hollow cylinder filled with valuable diamonds. The melodramatic incidents of this story are set in a lush Southern atmosphere of "mockingbird singing on the crest of a tall magnolia."

Of the sketches of the Civil War "The Maid of Jasmindale" is representative. Here the sweetheart of a recently returned Confederate artilleryman overhears him reminiscing with a fellow veteran about their prize gun, "Annie." This leads to inevitable misunderstanding, and after much ado:

> He looked at the girl. He saw it all now. "Annie!" he knelt at her side and put his arm around her. "And you were jealous of a gun!"
> And the mocking-bird in the jasmine-vine above them burst into a carol of love to its mate.

Perhaps the most durable feature of these tales is their settings. Peck seems to have a sort of embryo plan of staking out a literary locality. Over half of the sketches are set in Oakville and Oak County, which are, of course, thin disguises for Tuscaloosa and the surrounding county. In "The Trouble at St. James's," for example, St. James Episcopal Church with its bell tower covered with the scarlet trumpet vine is

Christ Church, Tuscaloosa's most historic sanctuary. Although some of Peck's landscapes are conventional with standard Southern props—magnolias and mockingbirds, katydids and cape jasmines, and plowhands chanting plantation songs—many of the settings contain his best writing, especially when he is not obviously striving to be "literary." In fact, some of Peck's best prose describes in straightforward, simple style a bicycle tour that he and Frank W. Chandler took through France. These accounts appeared as a series in the New Orleans *Times-Democrat,* about 1895—the dates of the clippings being removed when Peck pasted them in a booklet, entitled "Wheeling Abroad," for possible future publication.

The same descriptive skill evidenced in his travel essays appears in "Pap's Mules." When he describes the children's delight in hiding the mules from Federal scouts in the familiar woods and creeks below their farm, he writes with a simple joy that marks his best prose:

> Reaching the morass, overshadowed by great gum and cypress trees and dotted with tufts of watergrass, she leaped from hillock to hillock over the black mud.
> She stopped a moment to listen. She heard nothing but the hammering of a logcock on a dead gum-tree, and the tiny bark of a squirrel.

And when in "Hamilton's Ruse" Peck writes of the heat on the "Jimson and Coffee weeds" near the old ruined paper mill, his atmosphere is authentic and memorable.

Another notable feature of Peck's stories is the Negro dialect. Usually reasonably realistic, it is not overdone like much of the dialect fiction of the nineties. "The Trouble at St. James's" is related by the Negro sexton Dan, who recalls an Easter rendition of the "Hallelujah Chorus":

> De spranners hallelujahed high up in de trebles, den de basses roared hit down low, and de 'traltos an' de tenors pitched hit

back an' forth in de middle; den dey all sot in an' shouted hit
together, an' seesawed an' zig-zagged up an' down de scales, while
de organist played wid his all fours, an ever' stop pulled out to de
very een.

A single line of Negro dialect is occasionally the best moment
of an entire sketch. In "The Old Piano," an unconvincing and
over-sentimental tale of a poverty-stricken music teacher, the
maid Hannah is sent out to pawn the last of the family silver,
for Miss Peyton and the faithful Hannah must eat. But
Hannah goes on her mission most reluctantly, muttering:
"I'se a-consumin' wid shame. I'se des eatin' up all de Peyton
silber."

Of character creation in these tales there is little, and that
little is usually found among the minor dramatis personae,
particularly among the Negroes like old Dan in "The Trouble
at St. James's" and Uncle Ben and Aunt Martha in
"Nobody's Property." The plots are often outworn, and the
surprises are rarely effective. In "Sister Taylor's Registered
Letter" the reader has long ago guessed that finally the
widow's inquisitive son will emerge in his mother's sunbonnet
and sign for the letter that his mother has refused, much to
the annoyance of the village gossipers. The letter turns out to
contain a gift of two hundred dollars.

The tales, moreover, are rarely concerned with theme even
in a broad sense; they are frankly incidents that only occasionally reflect a meaningful comment on a way of life. As
stories that depend upon setting and surprising turns of
events for their effectiveness, the tales offer little evidence
that Peck was concerned with point of view or authority for
conveying the narrative. Almost all the sketches are related
from the omniscient perspective without much thought as to
the continued convincingness of this method. Even when the
first-person narrator is used, as in "The Trouble at St.
James's," the speaker soon becomes omniscient rather than
humanly limited from his personal point of view.

Like many of the nineteenth-century fiction writers in both England and the United States, Peck seems to have looked upon the sketch as a mere stepping stone to higher things. After publishing *Alabama Sketches* (1902), he turned his energies to novel writing. With the short stories Peck at least had reasonable success in marketing his work. With the novel, however, he had no success except with magazine serialization of novelettes like "Nobody's Property." Among his literary remains are such novel-length manuscripts as "Over the Wind-Mill" (225 typed pages), "The Mating of Margaret" (216 typed pages), "Old Free Nancy" (178 typed pages), and a Civil War adventure story with its title page missing (210 typed pages). None of these novels was ever printed. As the letters of rejection still attached to some of the returned manuscripts indicate, the publishers found them smooth and appealing, vapid and over-sentimental for an age that liked its sentimentality.

Despite its obvious shortcomings Peck's career in prose fiction is both interesting and unusual. Occasionally, when the outlines of the tale are simple and credible, particularly in the Civil War stories like "Nobody's Property" and "Pap's Mules," there is real promise. Whether this promise was fulfilled or not, Peck is unique in the Alabama literary scene of his day. Except for John Trotwood Moore, who wrote about a half dozen stories with settings in the Alabama Black Belt and planned but never published a volume of "Songs and Stories of Alabama" as a companion to his *Songs and Stories of Tennessee,* Samuel Minturn Peck was the only writer of short stories at the turn of the century giving any serious attention to re-creating the Alabama of Civil War, Reconstruction, and contemporary times.

In his latter days Peck rarely referred to his prose. In interviews and personal letters it appears to be a closed chapter, for he took increasing refuge in the belief that he was primarily a poet. In his prose he had aspired to be the James Lane Allen, the Joel Chandler Harris, or the Thomas Nelson

Page of Alabama, but he never quite succeeded. He could never find around him in the Alabama of his day any of the earlier literary enthusiasm that fellowship and common interests made possible among A.B. Meek, F.A.P. Barnard, Thomas Maxwell, and William Russell Smith with their youthful journals, the *Bachelor's Button* and the *Southron.* This was the happy freshness of an early world that centered around the first years of the University of Alabama—the kind of literary companionship that the young E.A. Poe sought at the University of Virginia and could not remain long enough to find. But these high-spirited days belonged to the generation before Peck. His formative years were spent in Tuscaloosa—in the shadow of the University of Alabama— during post-Civil War days of poverty and decadence. To a certain extent it might be said that his genteel dilettantism was predestined. Nevertheless, Samuel Minturn Peck, with all his apparent failings, is the best measure in fiction and poetry of a man of letters that Alabama had produced before World War I.

5

Some in Addition: The Uncollected Stories of William March

WHEN William March died in 1954, he had written six novels: *Company K* (1933), *Come In at the Door* (1934), *The Tallons* (1936), *The Looking-Glass* (1943), *October Island* (1952), and *The Bad Seed* (1954). He had recently laid aside another, "The Practiced Hand," which was about one-third written, because he believed he had discovered a better way to tell a story of juvenile delinquency. He began again, changing the boy whose father had been a policeman to a little girl named Rhoda. After *The Bad Seed* was finished, he wrote one of his sisters: "There are five more books I want to do."

Though most of his energy since 1947, when he returned South to recover from a mental state of black depression, had gone toward novel writing, William March had never permanently put aside his life-long interest in the short story. In his early teens he had written poetry, begun a long novel, and finished several stories like "There Fate Is Hell" and "Bet's Bravery," written about 1908. In February 1954 he had published his last, "The Bird House." In between these dates he had compiled three collections of short stories—*The Little Wife and Other Stories* (1935), *Some Like Them Short* (1939), and *Trial Balance: The Collected Short Stories* (1945); this last collection contained fifty-five stories, twenty-two being new ones not in either of the previous two collections. He had told several friends of his intention to bring the total to one hundred before he died.

In addition to novels and short stories March had worked all during the 1930's on his "hundred fables," as he called them. This was the longest single manuscript among his papers when he died. He had first assembled the collection "about 1938," when he resigned his vice-presidency in the Waterman Steamship Corporation and settled down in a Manhattan apartment "to write as I please." At that time the manuscript contained about 125 fables, forty-five of which he published in various "little" magazines and quarterlies and in New York newspapers. During the 1940's he reworked them and discarded all but ninety-nine. A few years before his death, about the time he was moving from Mobile to New Orleans and considering buying in the Vieux Carré the first house he ever owned, March went through all his papers and rediscovered his book of fables. He found them "too good to destroy," as he frequently did with old papers and files, so he reworked them once again. The *99 Fables* was published posthumously in 1960 by The University of Alabama Press, as he would have wished.

William March was really two men. As William March—the name fate selected for him when the story bearing this name was accepted instead of two others with other pen names—he was a writer of fiction highly respected by many of the expert craftsmen of a new generation and by many ordinary readers who seemed unable to forget his stories. In 1954 Alistair Cooke of the Manchester *Guardian* called him "the most underrated of all contemporary American writers of fiction." As William Edward Campbell he was born in 1893 in Mobile, the eldest son and second child of a large family. His early years were spent in the small sawmill towns of west Florida and south Alabama. When the family moved from Yellow Pine, to Pensacola, to Lockhart, he had already completed the "Intermediate Department"—the extent of Lockhart's schooling; so "Billy Campbell," who had just won five dollars in a National Oats jingle contest, went to work in a lumber mill as did Jim Tallon in the novel *The Tallons.* At sixteen he took a business course in Mobile; at nineteen he and a friend ventured north for a year to attend Valparaiso University in Indiana. Having exhausted his funds, he worked in Mobile again until he saved enough to devote 1914-1915 to the study of law at the University of Alabama. When his funds again ran out, he went to New York and worked as law clerk and subpoena server.

In 1917 when the United States entered the World War, William E. Campbell immediately joined the Marines, participated in all the bitter fighting of his 5th Regiment, 43rd Company—Mont Blanc, Soissons, Verdun, Belleau Wood—and received almost every award for personal bravery including a Distinguished Service Cross, Navy Cross, and Croix de guerre. "As a result of wounds I received in action," he wrote in 1932, "I shall never be entirely well again so long as I live"— wounds to the body and to the psyche as well.

After the war he returned to Mobile and worked with Waterman, helping to organize the Mobile home office, traveling over the East and Midwest to "solicit freight," and putting three times the money he took out as salary back into the company. Then came the years in Europe: the depressive atmosphere in Hamburg as he watched Hitler's rise to power (so well depicted in "Personal Letter") and the more pleasant though uneasy days in London from 1935 to 1937 (reflected in "Sweet, Who Was the Armourer's Maid" and "A Short History of England") when he knew such writers as Elizabeth Bowen, H.E. Bates, and Stephen Spender.

Almost all of these experiences had already found some expression in the novels and short stories of these busy years. On trains, in hotels and apartments, in little towns and big cities, William March had always found time to read and to write. From the days of his schoolboy interest in composing verse and fiction he had come to know creative writing as a pleasure as well as a sort of necessary therapy. His first important story, "The Holly Wreath," had appeared in the October *Forum* of 1929, and using his World War letter-diary (sent from France to his older sister Margaret), he had re-created his war experiences in the powerful *Company K.* The growing to manhood of a boy in south Alabama is the theme of *Come In at the Door;* and while he was working in Germany and England he recalled the environment of Lockhart, Alabama, and his work in the sawmill. This village he had renamed Hodgetown in *The Tallons*—the dramatic story of two brothers, a farmer and a mill worker, both in love with the same girl.

In addition to these novels, his short stories had appeared in leading magazines and in *The O. Henry Prize Stories* and *The Best American Short Stories;* and *The Little Wife and Other Stories* had been collected in 1935. Late in 1938 he had a second volume of short stories ready, *Some Like Them Short.* It was about this year that he decided to give more time to writing, and from 1938 to 1954 William March was in the ascendancy over William E. Campbell.

When he died in New Orleans, March was a wealthy bachelor who had grown tired of New York life with its hurry and bustle, its literary teas, cocktail parties, and professional chit-chat, though he still continued to write occasionally to literary friends like Harnett T. Kane, Carson McCullers, and Paul Engle. He lived quietly surrounded by one of the finest collections of modern French paintings in private hands. Perls Galleries in New York issued a special catalogue for the exhibition and sale of "The William March Collection" from October 4 to November 13, 1954, as ordered by the executors of the estate. Paintings by Picasso, Bombois, Klee, Roualt, Soutine, Utrillo, Vlaminck, and others attest the taste and skill with which across the years the collection had been assembled.

The statement that he wanted to write a hundred short stories worth preserving was not an idle boast. Among

March's papers is a list of the titles for the unwritten balance; he was always fascinated by titles and usually began with one, though occasionally he changed it along the way of the writing or when the story went from magazine to collected volume. Some of the unwritten stories were to have these titles: "Man Who Died in My Bed," "Broad Jump," Presbyterian Picnic," "Straight Man," "Thank Everybody," "It's His Wife," "Beloved Loss," "Happy Ending," "Measuring John," "Great Banana Crisis," "From a Distance," "Big Chance," "At Mrs. Cotton's," "Jury Room," "Gold-Tooth Andy." For some of these March left the outline of the plot or the statement of the central idea. Three examples are the following:

The Blue Envelope

Postman delivers letter to John—Sara, his wife, opens it, feeling something strange in letter, obviously from a woman, ambiguous. Husband calls & asks if letter received. She says no. Seals up letter again. Makes it appear that postman has dropped it in street. Remails it. Next day the letter comes & husband gets it. Wife waits for him to explain. He doesn't. She is precluded from ever asking about the letter. Hates husband—etc.

Swing Low

The Negroes before Civil War working in fields. The formation of clouds. The talk reveals them. They talk of freedom. The cloud becomes a chariot: Pearl River used first then Jordan. "Swing low, sweet chariot," Jupe says. They stop work. All begin to sing. Observer stops them.

Oldest Little Boy in the World

On his fiftieth birthday his mother celebrates their golden wedding anniversary—jokingly of course. He's never had a sweetheart. His mother has always been everything to him.

Along with these plans for possible future stories March was thriftily keeping copies of his published ones in a folder with a few corrections penned in against the day of a new volume. Not under the pressure of living by his writing, he worked carefully over his stories and let his literary agent— first Max Lieber, later Harold Ober Associates—place them. He did not like the idea of "slanting" his fiction so that it would be marketable for a particular magazine. In 1932 he wrote his sister Margaret: "I had another offer from the *Saturday Evening Post* not so long ago and one from *Collier's,* also a tentative bid from *Cosmopolitan,* all of which I turned down politely. They merely wrote asking me to do something for them in their manner, but you know what that means. I'd druther solicit freight." Earlier, in 1930, he had written: "I almost sold another story to *Forum* the other day. It was recommended by everybody until it got to the editor, Henry Goddard Leach himself, who rejected it. This is the second time he's done that. He feels that I'm 'unhealthy and decadent'—which is probably true, but who cares? Literature isn't produced by happy, uncomplicated souls. I don't particularly care. If I'm any good, I'll find my place some day, if I'm not, it doesn't matter much." Once March had finished a story, however, and published it (even in a "little" magazine that had no funds to pay for its pieces), he was sure to put it in a collected edition. The only stories omitted from the three collections are those that had been expanded into novels. In this respect March was quite different from Scott Fitzgerald, whose work also alternated between novel and short story. Because he always needed large sums of money, Fitzgerald wrote his short stories primarily for the *Saturday Evening Post,* but when he issued his collections he limited them severely to what he considered his best work.

It is not surprising, then, that March, after the 1945 volume, had been preparing another that would probably have contained the majority of the following stories:

1. Nine Prisoners [*Forum,* December, 1931; *Some Like Them Short* (1939), 4200 words], [c. 1930]

2. The Unploughed Patch [*Pagany*, October-March, 1932-33, 24,500 words], [c. 1931]
3. The Marriage of the Bishops [*Accent*, Autumn, 1940, 2400 words], 1940
4. A Great Town for Characters [*Esquire*, May 1946, 3600 words], 1945
5. Ballet of the Bowie Knives [*Cross Section*, 1947, 3300 words], 1945.
6. First [unpublished, 2000 words], 1945
7. One-Way Ticket [*Good Housekeeping*, January, 1946, 4000 words], 1945
8. History of the Credulous Widow ...[*Ladies' Home Journal*, October, 1948, 100 words], 1946
9. Old Sorority Sister [*Collier's*, September 28, 1946, 5300 words], 1946
10. October Island [*Good Housekeeping*, October, 1946, 9400 words], 1946
11. The Bird House [*Ellery Queen's Mystery Magazine*, February, 1954, 5500 words], 1946
12. The Red Jacket [unpublished, 5500 words], 1946
13. The Long Pursuit [unpublished, 2900 words], 1946

The information in the brackets indicates the source of the initial publication of each story and the approximate number of words. The date following is that of composition, as indicated in the author's notes.

Except for the first three, these stories are the ones March had written since *Trial Balance* in 1945 up to the time of his physical breakdown in 1947 and his return South. From this period until his death his principal creative energy went into novels: *October Island*, the unfinished "The Practiced Hand," and *The Bad Seed*.

The first three need special comment to justify their inclusion in the list of uncollected stories. "Nine Prisoners," first appearing in the December *Forum* of 1931, was collected in *Some Like Them Short,* though March had omitted it from *The Little Wife and Other Stories* probably because it was used as the single most sustained dramatic episode (in a slightly altered version) in *Company K.* For some unexplained reason it was the only story from the first two volumes, then both out of print, that was omitted from the collected stories, *Trial Balance.* It is restored in this list because it is one of March's best, and if the uncollected group is to complement the "Collected Stories," it must be present even though "Fifteen from Company K," "Two Soldiers," "Sixteen and the Unknown Soldier," "Dappled Fawn," "Private Edward Romano," and other parts of the novel *Company K* that once appeared as individual stories are here omitted. The relationship is like that of the sonnets of a sonnet sequence, which March once experimented with writing; they can be read, understood, and enjoyed as separate entities, but their true significance is best perceived when they are read sequentially in the whole work. "Nine Prisoners," however, is a slightly different case. It is almost as well known as the novel, having appeared in numerous anthologies not edited by March and having been widely commented upon. Professor N. Bryllion Fagin in *America through the Short Story* begins his list of the best writers of World War I stories, including Thomas Boyd, Lawrence Stallings, Leonard Nason, and others, with the name of William March. "'Nine Prisoners,'" he writes, "attracted wide attention by its power and unusualness, and many letters, some attacking and some defending" the validity and realism of its central idea were received by the editors of *Forum.* What Stephen Crane did for the Civil War in sections of *The Red Badge of Courage,* March has done for World War I. He succeeds in "Nine Prisoners," as he had hoped he would, in making the men and their reactions universal in implication, and encouraged by its impact he proceeded with a novel in similar vein. But "Nine Prisoners" differs from the other segments of *Company K* in the theme underscored by its title: those who plan and participate in atrocities to war prisoners become themselves prisoners. The bold irony of the title of the short story is lost in the rearrangement of the material in the novel, where the last section spoken by Private James Wade is considerably expanded and placed in the mouth of Private Joseph Delaney, who is assigned the prologue of the 113-man "Roster" of speakers. The other separate publications are not significantly altered in the novel, which itself might be called a collection of 113 short stories if it were not for the total unity of the sequence. For all these reasons, therefore, "Nine Prisoners" needs to be restored to the March canon.

"The Unploughed Patch," first published in *Pagany* in 1933, perhaps because it was later reworked into *The Tallons,* was also omitted from previous collections. But this first version of a twice-told tale deserves to be remembered. For uncompromising realistic tragedy it stands among March's most memorable tales, and among his many unattractive women Hallie Barrows, as she is called in this version, is a true Southern mill-town Emma Bovary. Written before March's passion for Jung and Freud, and unencumbered with too much landscape used as objective correlative, the story is in many ways more moving than the novel it fathered. Though it is a rather long story in its original form (about 24,500 words), it is compressed into "one Saturday afternoon in June" when Andrew Tallon pays his regular weekly visit to Gramlings store. On the way he rehearses the longings and defeats of his life, thwarted as he is by his disfiguring hairlip. He tries vainly to forget the body of his brother Jim buried in the "unploughed patch." He now finds his life not simpler, as he had hoped, but more complicated. All he is sure of is that the sky is "deeply blue—all one color." The neat compressed frame is sacrificed in the novel, and the apprehension of Andrew in the end weakens the novel's main idea of fraternal love and hate. A perceptive Philadelphia *Record* reviewer of *The Tallons*—he had probably not seen

"The Unploughed Patch" in *Pagany,* a short-lived "little" magazine of limited circulation—wrote: "Its plot might have been telescoped into a powerful long short-story. But there is a lot in its background that I would not have missed, for Mr. March is a quiet, subtle and rather devilish interpreter of the Southern scene."

This same comment might well be made about the South Pacific novel, *October Island.* It gains little in impact or total meaning in its expanded form, but some splendid scenes with the heroine's sister Lurline in Mobile and New Orleans would be hard to sacrifice. In fact, these three stories—"Nine Prisoners," "The Unploughed Patch," and "October Island"— provide fascinating studies in the art that Guy de Maupassant so much admired, that of retelling stories on different scales. What Somerset Maugham found true of Maupassant's experimentation with *The Legacy* is applicable also to March's versions: "I think no one can read the two versions without admitting that in the first there is not a word too little and in the second not a word too much."

"The Marriage of the Bishops," first printed in *Accent* in 1940, was probably omitted from *Trial Balance* because it was originally planned as one of the "hundred fables." When these were finally finished and tentatively titled "Ninety-Nine Fables," "The Marriage of the Bishops" was far longer than the others, and perhaps it was excluded to give the manuscript volume a certain unity of proportion. The fable is an excellent one and if included would have added considerably to the background about the land of the Bretts and Wittins. The warmly human Bishop of the Wittins and his dislike for the Bishop of the Bretts is no more rational than Tom Brown's dislike of Dr. Fell, who later himself became a Bishop of Oxford; but because the situation is so sharply drawn with the Bishop of the Bretts speaking platitudes and cracking his knuckles one by one, our sympathies are with the Wittin despite his recent denial of divorces to his subjects who "disliked" their wives. Now that the irony pinches his own ecclesiastical foot in a symbolic marriage for the duration of the winter with the Brett, we feel for him and for our irrational selves as he falls back into the waiting arms of his rival, who exclaims, " . . . in his cheerful, irritating voice, 'Just relax more! . . . That's all you need!' "

This baker's dozen of stories is more than a listing of March's posthumous fictional remains. They are, for the most part, the pieces he himself designated for an additional volume as well as those he had omitted not for reasons of their quality, but for reasons that seemed wise when his plans as a writer of long fiction were still unfolding.

These last stories also represent many of March's interests and form a kind of final fictional testimony of the man whom Maxwell Geismar has recently referred to as a "literary unconscious" of his time—"one of these gifted artists who never quite achieved his due during the Nineteen Thirties and Forties." Like William Faulkner, March created a mythical county that can be mapped like Yoknapatawpha. Better than any other Southerner, March has described in his Pearl County and Reedyville the milieu of the small towns and sawmill villages of south Alabama and west Florida that he knew so well. This listing adds three new tales to his saga: "The Unploughed Patch," "The Long Pursuit," and "The Red Jacket." The last is a sensitive account of an adolescent's first awareness of the nature and meaning of love. Based on an incident from his boyhood days in Lockhart, Alabama, the story is unique among all March's fiction: its approach to love is simple, honest, and almost sentimental instead of ironic and brutal; and Mrs. Madison is one of March's few understanding women and his only successful attempt to draw the equivocal feminine psyche.

"The Long Pursuit" is the only "unfinished" tale in the listing—and that only in the last page or so where the author has sketched the action and even suggested the key phrases of dialogue. ("The Long Run of Riley" has not been included even though a first draft is completely finished; it lacks considerable work on the problem of focus in the dying convict's mind.) "The Long Pursuit" is the last of the Reedyville stories, and it is a good tall tale of rural humor. Told by Mrs. Kent, that voluble historian of Pearl County, the story is a worthy companion to her notorious "Borax Bottle." Again Mamie, the cook, hides "just inside the door hemming dish towels" so that she won't miss any details. Mrs. Kent, sitting as usual on her front porch waiting for a likely listener, especially when the doctor is out on call, is always a slightly ribald raconteur in the grand manner. This time her theme, like that of the Wife of Bath, is love and marriage: "It has always seemed peculiar to me that when a man is so repugnant that the idea of his touching a woman throws her into hysterics, the only way to solve the situation is to marry him to her, so that he will be legally entitled to touch her as often as he pleases, but there are so many of the conventions I don't pretend to understand."

March's days as an apprentice lawyer and process server in New York before he enlisted in the Marines are echoed nowhere else except in "Old Sorority Sister." Here he defines the cruel beauty of a mean job too well done and depicts again with satirical gusto the successful woman writer that he skillfully employed in the person of Minnie MacInnis McMinn in *The Looking-Glass.*

March's experience as a fighting Marine finds expression in "Nine Prisoners," though he attempts to generalize the situation; "it is futile and it is hopeless," he wrote, "for any man who has actually served on the line to attempt to make well-meaning romantic folk share his knowledge; there is, simply, no common denominator." In "The Ballet of the Bowie Knives" March has recalled another incident from World War I, this time broad and earthy in its humor and ironically recollected in the feverish atmosphere of World War II. At a shoe shine stand in Grand Central Station three counterparts—two generations of fighting men, civilian and old soldier, and timidity and braggadocio—are all suspended in momentary juxtaposition.

In "The Marriage of the Bishops" and "October Island" March has expressed his long concern about Christian ethics, especially as they are interpreted by ministers and missionaries—a point of view he shared with many of his literary contemporaries like Sinclair Lewis, F. Scott Fitzgerald, and Ernest Hemingway. In "The Marriage of the Bishops" he approaches the problem in fable form, giving a homely illustration of a bishop's lack of charitable perception—the same point he was making in other fables written about the same time and in earlier stories, like "Mist on the Meadow" with Brother Hightower as a central character. In "The World and Its Redeemers," for example, the fable concludes with this moral: "The world could have been saved long ago if it had not been for its redeemers." In "October Island" he again attacks narrow militant Christianity, a matter that may hark back to memories of his strong-minded grandfather March from whose family name the pen name March was derived. In going through some old letters in 1941 William wrote one of his sisters, "Grandpa's letter to you is a masterpiece of religious mania. I wonder how much that sort of thing affected your own attitude." Actually the *Good Housekeeping* version is in some ways more sharply ironic than the novel as it deals with the cruelly comic process of a missionary's wife becoming a pagan mother-goddess and rather liking it. In the short story her violent death is foreshadowed, but in the novel she goes on triumphantly.

"One-Way Ticket" reflects March's deep interest in psychoanalysis. Written from the point of view of Dr. Brackett, the story unfolds with a somewhat double implication and obliquely recalls the days of his residence in England and his friendship with Dr. Edward Glover, who once said that William March taught him more by his idle fantasies than all his books and years of practice had done.

"The Bird House" also contains a psychiatrist, a woman, probably modeled on Dr. Clara Happel, a German analyst whom March helped to settle in this country. The story reflects his fascination with the murder mystery, which he indulged at length in *The Bad Seed.* In "The Bird House" he has taken the notorious Isadore Fink case and allowed a psychiatrist, a poet, a lawyer, and a publisher to solve it, each in his own way. The setting is reminiscent of March's former New York apartment equipped with his actual Filipino houseboy formerly employed by Jimmy Walker.

These last stories echo many of the interests of William March and draw upon the variety of people and places that made up the eventful life of William Edward Campbell.

As short stories these thirteen reenforce March's theories about this form of fiction. In length they range from 24,500 to 9,400, to less than 100 words. "The Unploughed Patch" and "October Island" belong to the genre of the novelette that has attracted most American writers of fiction from Poe, Melville, and James to Faulkner, Katherine Anne Porter, and Eudora Welty. "History of the Credulous Widow . . ." the editor of the *Ladies' Home Journal* printed as "Untitled Story—by William March" and explained to its readers: "At a recent party in New York, William March, favorite author of the 'butcher paper' literary critics, contended that he had authored the 'shortest short story ever written.'" In preparing it for reprinting March equipped it with a comically long title: "History of the Credulous Widow Who Met an Admiring Stranger in a Cocktail Lounge, and Who after Turning Her Liquid Assets Over to Him, Was Never Seen Again by Her Friends," a title that satirizes the too clever, neat appellations of popular fiction, perhaps even his own penchant for the deceptively ironic title, like "A Sum in Addition," "Personal Letter," and "A Short History of England." The text of the story, in contrast, reads as follows:

On Monday she was in his thoughts.
On Tuesday she was in his automobile.
On Wednesday she was in his hotel room.
On Thursday she was in his arms.
On Friday she was in his big wardrobe trunk, checked through
to Los Angeles.

No one can deny that for a murder mystery this is clearer and simpler than "The Bird House" or *The Bad Seed.*

In this group of stories there is considerable evidence that March still believes that a story must have a plot at its heart— something must happen. Although he has experimented with the sketch of tone and atmosphere, as in "The Pattern That Gulls Weave," he has most often held to the concept that incident makes life, and man's reaction to other men and incidents constitutes idea. "A Great Town for Characters" has a murder as its central incident, but its theme about the provincial meaning of manhood is ironically never apparent to the merchant who narrates the incident.

The "oral" tradition of a narrator, which March likes to employ, while it seems to clutter the telling, actually achieves the economy that makes his work most distinctive to the perceptive reader and at the same time grounds it in the oldest of folklore ways. William March was himself a great raconteur: having conceived the germ of his story, he liked to tell it to any and all who would listen. And many did, for the man always had the spell-binding charm of a youthful ancient mariner. If the story went poorly in one frame, he would try another next time. Of the stories in this listing "A Great Town for Characters," "Ballet of the Bowie Knives," "The Red Jacket," and "The Long Pursuit" illustrate this technique of multiple-level writing through the use of a narrator. "Nine Prisoners" poses nine points of view and nine tellers of a central incident.

His insistence on a core of plot has naturally led March toward the fable and legend. In addition to "The Marriage of the Bishops," which was planned in the Aesopian style of the

99 Fables, "First" recounts the biblical story of Cain and Abel, but from Cain's point of view and from a perspective of time. This strangely exciting and disturbing story, along with "The Red Jacket" and "The Long Pursuit," has never been published.

Because of his insistence on plot and because of his favorite theme of the ironic cruelty of life, William March found himself out of favor with the American critics of the late 1930's and early 1940's—he fared better in England. Now perhaps he can begin to take his rightful place as a significant writer of fiction in the years between two world wars. His style has always aimed at clarity devoid of mannerism. He has eschewed the staccato sharpness of Hemingway and the baroque eloquence of Faulkner. He believed from the beginning that his generation was no more "lost" than other generations, but that it must seek out and acknowledge the root of the grim cruelty that lies at the heart of human life. Much of his fiction has concerned violence, but never violence for the sake of violence. Much of his fiction has been set in the South, but never has he worn his Southernism with a vengeance. When Bruce Lankester in "The Red Jacket" writes a poem about the oleander bush on the old Porterfield place and later goes to the cemetery to see Mrs. Madison's grave behind Mattie Tatum's monument to her mother, the reader of the Reedyville stories is immediately drawn back into his old haunts. But Reedyville, he well knows, is every little town full of "characters"—not an assortment of mere pathological case studies—just as March's World War I is every war. It is his sanity of style and insistence on the normal abnormality of us all that will finally win William March his permanent place in American literature. These uncollected stories, long and short, uniquely representative of March's style, interests, and ideas, must now stand in place of all the thirty-odd tales he planned and did not live to write.

When March died suddenly in the spring of 1954 Robert Tallant wrote in the *Saturday Review* that there was a sheet of paper in the famous author's typewriter headed "Poor Pilgrim, Poor Stranger," which reads as follows:

The time comes in the life of each of us when we realize that death awaits us as it awaits others, that we will receive at the end neither preference not exemption. It is then, in that disturbed moment, that we know life is an adventure with an ending, not a succession of bright days that go on forever. Sometimes the knowledge comes with repudiation and quick revolt that such injustice awaits us, sometimes with fear that dries the mouth and closes the eyes for an instant, sometimes with servile weariness, and acquiescence more dreadful than fear. The knowledge that my own end was near came with pain, and afterwards with astonishment; with the conventional heart attack, from which, I've been told, I've made an excellent recovery.

It may be as Mr. Tallant suggests that William March was describing "as well as any man can, his reactions to his own death." It may also be that as a writer of fiction who had experienced a first coronary thrombosis several months earlier he was beginning another story about a person like himself and like all of us who are poor pilgrims, poor strangers in this life.

6

William March's Alabama

MANY writers from Joseph G. Baldwin to Harper Lee have used the Alabama scene as background for their stories, but no single writer has executed so broad a canvas of the state as has William March (1893-1945). Not only as background has Alabama served him; he has faithfully and artistically recorded the dialects and temper of many of her people and regions from the turn of the century to the 1940's. He has described the decay of a plantation like that of the Hurrys— the whites and Negroes who destroy and at the same time preserve it. In his novels about the Tallons and the Tarletons of Pearl County, March has depicted the depressing environment of the farms, mill towns, and crossroad stores that typify much of the southern half of the state. In the Reedyville stories and *The Looking-Glass* he has drawn with sympathy and irony the life of a small Alabama county seat: its bankers, doctors, teachers, ministers, lawyers, boarding-house keepers, prostitutes, pool-room operators, business-men, journalists, and photographers. He has written accurately of the Negroes and the injustices done them by mobs like the one that castrated Driver in "Happy Jack." He has told of the dull goodness of farm wives like Effie Cleaver in *The Tallons* with her ever-increasing brood of children, and he has defined with painful clarity the brilliant misfits like Manny Nelloha and Rance Palmiller, whose families and friends alike cannot begin to understand them. The unusual and the run-of-the-mill—this balance that is human life—has made William March's fiction take on the classic quality of an Alabama microcosm that is in reality a world macrocosm.

Though the time span in March's South Alabama fiction is shorter than that of Faulkner's North Mississippi from Indian days to the present, March's geographic scope is somewhat broader and his cross sections of the human spectrum are perhaps more varied. The Hurry plantation on the edge of Athlestan is not far from the Gulf of Mexico, while Pearl County with its rivers, woods, farms, and towns nearer the center of the state is as well mapped as Yoknapatawpha. And the three major cities of the state—Birmingham, Mobile, and Montgomery—all appear in March's six novels and sixty-odd short stories. The human scene includes the maladjusted and degenerates, the average well-meaning middle class, as well as the self-styled aristocrats of land or purse. Without doing violence to his various aesthetic purposes and methods of storytelling, William March, better than any other writer of American fiction, has spread before his readers the state of Alabama: the land and the people of its plantations, small farms, crossroads stores, sawmills, county seats, and cities.

During the last years of the nineteenth century the Hurry plantation in *Come In at the Door* (1934) has fallen into disrepair. After the death of his wife Ellen Tarleton, whose forebears were crossroads storekeepers and small farmers of sturdy self-righteous bent, Robert Hurry, hope and scion of the plantation, has slipped into the subtle spell of easy decadence; as a relatively young man he is disintegrating morally, physically, and spiritually. The plantation Negroes, however, are more enduring; Mitty and Hattie, Jim and Baptiste—all vie for the heart of the lonely boy Chester, the product of plantation aristocracy and middle-class yeomanry. Robert now only hunts and sits sullenly on his sagging columned veranda, while he should be practicing law in Athlestan as his mother had hoped by putting the last of the family funds into his education at the University of Alabama. The only enthusiasm that the remaining Negroes and whites on the plantation share is the endless charm of the Alabama woods, rivers, and fields. When Mitty and Chester go down to the river to bring clean sand for the kitchen floor, they

> would often sit quietly . . . on the bluff above the rotted landing, and watch the colored river and the strange unhappy birds blown inland from the sea . . . . The sand here was not white and dead, like the sand that fringed the Gulf, but was richer in color: a pale gold of the texture and shade of yellow cornmeal . . . . The trees which were tallest were so dark against the sky that they seemed at this distance not green at all, but rather the rich purple of Caesars.

When Chester and Baptiste went for a walk after their morning tutorial sessions, where Baptiste is always addressed as Professor Simon, they

> passed through . . . an old field, worn out and abandoned, in which wire-grass and weeds grew. The rails which once enclosed it had rotted away . . . . At the edge of the field . . . was a persimmon tree loaded with ripe, lavender fruit . . . A covey of quail, walking with exact, delicate steps, passed near them across the open space between the woods and the field, opening and closing their bright eyes.

This rural atmosphere is spellbinding, and after years of adolescence in the Tarleton home and of marriage to Abbie in Bay City, Chester finally comes, after his father's burial at the end of the novel, to a partial understanding of himself and "the cruelty [which] underlies everything and which will outlast everything that lives." Only when he returns to the fields and river he has known does he realize that the power of the storm, the cleanness of the sand, and the peace of the woods make for sanity of soul.

The town of Athlestan, on the other hand, is a sinister abode of the "moojer woman," whom Baptiste must seek to have her lift the "conjur" placed on him by Mitty's death mouth. The courthouse dominates the small town, and behind it is the jail, "a four-story building of red brick, towered and crenelated like some medieval castle, and with windows barred in thick iron." Years later Chester found Athlestan little changed. "There were the same wide streets with their double rows of oaks, the same somnolence, the same imperviousness to the outside world."

The Hurrys themselves are "the last of a family whose gentility had worn it out." Robert had "no aptitude for books, and he had felt lost and out of place at the university." He was weary of his mother's endless recital "of the past glories of the family: of the generals, the bishop and the governor which had come out of it, vigorous people who could manage not only their own destinies but the destinies of others." In the eyes of his mother he had married a "silly country belle," and now after the death of mother and wife Robert has taken his wife's faithful servant as his mistress. But the last link with his past, a respect for learning, is what draws him toward the wandering Baptiste, a Negro fluent in French and well traveled; to Baptiste he "found himself talking excitedly, eagerly, for the first time in many months."

When Chester returns home after his father's death, he sees from a distance that Mitty has had the house painted outside, but inside "the great living room, which had once been magnificent with carpets and chandeliers, was bare now of all furniture. The floor had been painted white and it was lined with a series of incubators and chicken brooders." Questioned by Chester, Mitty pathetically replies, "What else could I do . . . except what I done?"

For Chester the river now flows "sluggishly . . . into sullen eddies," the wharf has entirely gone, and there is nothing left except a few blackened pilings leaning unsteadily away from the current. The Negro cabin which had once been barrenly cheerful with summer whitewash or winter evening fire that the pet coon loved, has now "fallen to pieces with the years, its roof already caved in, its door hanging on broken hinges." For Chester and for the South a way of life was passing.

The Tarletons, on the other hand, are a different breed, managing as they do their farm, timber lands, and country store at the crossroads between Morgan Center and Reedyville. They are strongly motivated by Protestant middle-class piety and a depressing sense of duty. Miss Sarah Tarleton, the backbone and conscience of the family, always says grace at table, and at seventy-three she confides to her diary: "But I must stop all this philosophizing and get to work. Mrs. Herman Outerbridge has got the books of the Pearl County Ladies' Auxiliary in a fearful tangle and it is up to me to straighten them out again . . . . I do not know how this county would get along if it were not for me." There was little that Miss Sarah would not undertake. When Edna, the brightest of the Cleaver children in *The Tallons* (1936), has no one to teach her piano, Miss Sarah undertakes the job. "It was in the yellow house behind the store, where the Tarleton family lived, that Edna began her music lessons with Miss Sarah early in October. She had no talent whatever and Miss Sarah felt it her duty to tell her so plainly."

This sense of duty carries over into the second generation. When Miss Sarah's nephew Bushrod Tarleton hears that his slattern wife is planning to return to live with him in Bay City, his sister Lillian writes him a letter warning him of the consequences: "she feels that it is her duty to do so." Not only is family moralizing a matter of duty, but education—in the broad sense of that term—is also a matter of duty. Aunt Sarah undertakes Chester's neglected "education as a duty . . . but [is] surprised at the way he learned." Uncle Frank, Sarah's older brother, believes that his son Bush "would have made a fine scholar. It's too bad he wouldn't finish college . . . . Education is the greatest thing in the world."

But Aunt Sarah challenges that statement. Aided by Professor Drewery, the county schoolmaster, they argue that "honor is greater than everything else combined." And at the end of *Come In at the Door,* when Aunt Sarah meditates on her "educated" nephews and nieces, she wonders what Jesse, Lillian, or her grandnephew Chester "have gained by their intelligence. Are they happier than I? I think I can answer that question firmly in the negative. My long life has taught me one thing: we must accept with humble heart whatever comes our way and we must not expect too much."

This strong-willed morality dominates the spirit of the Tarletons. It produces doctors like Jesse who now lives in Atlanta, civic- and P.T.A.-minded matrons like Lillian in Reedyville, as well as dreamers like Bush and liberal-minded Communists of the 1930 vintage like Bessie in New York. But the crossroads store, their original source of income, remains unchanged. When Andrew Tallon comes round the bend of the road on a Saturday afternoon, he sees the familiar scene: "Men sat lazily on the steps of the store yawning in the bright sunlight, coughing, clearing their throats and spitting at intervals, their women standing apart, gossiping, while below them pigs grunted contentedly, imbedded in the hot dust."

To the south of the Tarletons' store "the smoke from the Hodgetown mill lay faint and undisturbed against the sky." To Bushrod, however, this was an unlovely sight, he loved his tract of virgin timber—he had never even permitted his trees to be boxed for turpentine. Only in an attempt to save his impossible marriage to Ruby did he finally consent to sell it to the Hodge brothers who were "after it again." Some of the farmers around Green Point who were used to their own rural ways—their Saturday night dances at the Wrenns and their Wednesday night prayer meetings—also disliked the Hodge brothers and "the new people the sawmill had brought into the county. The mill with its noise and its energy meant change and a passing of [old] security." But most of the small landholders—the Outerbridges, the Cornells, the Tallons—had given options on their timber. The county newspaper recorded:

> Those interested in the progress of Pearl County will be delighted to hear that our progressive citizens, Mr. Thompson Hodge and his brother, Mr. Russell Hodge, who have been quietly taking options on timber in this vicinity, have decided to go ahead with their project, having obtained the backing of Powerful Financial Interests in the East.

So Hodgetown came into being, named for the Hodge brothers "only because their many friends demanded it," as Frank Tarleton laughingly read from the paper. At first Hodgetown was "hideous with its copings and fluted woodwork and its canary-colored paint, but years of weather had toned it down." The streets had been named personally by Mrs. Thompson Hodge, "in honor of what she, at least, believed to be the names of individual Indian tribes": Calumet, Tecumseh, Wampum, Hiawatha. The houses that lined them were "ornate or simple to accord with the relative importance of their occupants . . . grouped together with a military exactness of distinction." Mr. Russell Hodge, president of the corporation, lived in

> a white house with gray trimmings. Across the street from him, on a less desirable lot, lived his brother, Thompson, in a gray house with white trimmings. The fact that these houses were not painted yellow and were slightly at variance with the general pattern of the place gave the occupants a certain distinction . . . which was precisely the impression the Hodge wives sought to create.

The Bickerstaffs from Georgia, like most of the sawmill

people, lived in a "somewhat battered two-story house" near the log pond. Butterbean vines screened the west side of the porch, and a row of red cannas bordered the front walk and the fence between them and the Macbeths. In the evenings the arc light cast a dim glare on the street corner while tired husbands sat, in undershirts and socks, on their front porches as their wives, like Birdie Calkins, shelled endless baskets of peas.

The social centers of the village were the church and the commissary. "On the third Sunday of every month the Reverend A.A. Butler left his congregation in Reedyville to shift for itself as best it could and came to Hodgetown to preach in the Interdenominational Church there." The villagers accepted Brother Butler as a fashionable preacher and were "willing to concede his intellectual godliness, but . . . they liked a fiercer preacher, one with greater threats for their sinfulness and with wider promises of salvation, at the end, to sweeten the direness of prophecy." When Andrew Tallon after much searching of soul walked down the aisle during the singing of Brother Butler's last hymn, he alone reaffirmed his faith.

The village commissary had a wide veranda, and inside were long mirrors and many bolts of cloth. In the rear was a soft-drink and ice cream stand where the young sports and their dates of the neighborhood like Jim Tallon, Myrtle Bickerstaff, Rafe Hall, and Eloise Batty spent their Saturday evenings making wisecracks and telling bawdy stories. The commissary itself stood at the edge of the village, and behind it were the Negro quarters on the marshy piece of land drained by the creek. Their home-made beer and sandwiches could be had at George Stratton's place, a gambling hangout for white men, and farther on down the Green Point road Mamie Jackson ran another place where there were always "a couple of young white ladies visiting."

Beside the commissary stood the company hotel, where Myrtle and Jim spent their wedding night after a hasty marriage on Saturday in Reedyville. Sunday morning when Myrtle's parents came to call they could all hear the noises of the dining room below with "the rattle of heavy china set heavily and the sound of ice being chipped and dropped into a water-cooler." Not far away from the hotel was the other eating establishment—Mrs. Foley's boarding house, run by the company for workingmen with no families. In the short story "Whistles" (1945) good-hearted Mrs. Foley cannot rest easy from her recent heart attack lest Ada the cook forget that Wednesday's smothered steak with tomato gravy won't do for George Patmore, who "can't eat tomatoes in no shape or form."

Hodgetown is dominated by the smoke, the black mill pond, the noisy planer mill where Jim Tallon sharpens saws in the loft overlooking the piles of tall, straight pine logs. The houses, the church, the commissary, and the very souls of the mill folk belong outright to the Hodge brothers and the tyranny of their mill whistles.

Athlestan, Tarleton's store, and Hodgetown are all in the hinterland of Reedyville that lies somewhere between Montgomery and Mobile. It appears as urban focal point in both *Come In at the Door* and *The Tallons* and as the setting for at least a dozen short stories. In a sense Reedyville is the "hero" of *The Looking-Glass* (1943), March's most ambitious novel that threads its way in and out of the lives of many of its inhabitants.

Reedyville is a typical South Alabama county seat with its Courthouse Square, its fashionable Reedy Avenue, its middle-class sidestreets, and its across-the-tracks slums. Minnie McInnis McMinn, the society "editress" of the *Courier* and local historian and novelist, believes that Reedyville grew up on the spot where DeSoto and Chief Tuscaloosa held their "famous meeting"—according at least to a document in the Wentworths' private library. However that may be, by the time of the Civil War Reedyville was a prosperous town in the midst of "nearby plantations," and by the end of nineteenth century it was deteriorating along with the Reedys themselves, whose ankles "thickened as their blood thinned."

When Millicent Wentworth Reedy married an obscure photographer much older than herself, she was "an ungainly girl" who already foreshadowed the obesity she was shortly to reach. Her aunt Mrs. Wentworth could not imagine why she had acted so hastily. As she remarked in Shepherd's Department Store to Mrs. Porterfield, the other *grande dame* of the town, "I'm sure [Millicent] would have had other admirers, possibly, if she'd waited!" But Mrs. Wentworth was scarcely a reliable judge in these matters since she had driven her own daughter insane by her repressive attitudes; she even believed it deplorable that her ancient friend Virginia Dunwoody Owen had been born on Conception Street in Mobile: "a name which always struck [her] as being in the worst possible taste." Yet when Violet Wynn, the town bawdy-house operator known locally as Mattress Mae, died, it was old Mrs. Wentworth who despite age and rheumatism attended the services, looking at no one, imperiously fortified by her pearl choker and silver-headed cane. "I came because it was my *duty* to come," she told Professor St. Joseph. "When I read the funeral notice in the *Courier,* I said to myself, 'They shall not bury the old creature alone. Some one must be there, in common decency.' "

In addition to the old-guard families of Reedy, Dunwoody, Wentworth, and Porterfield, the Lankesters were among the most prominent. While Clarence Lankester was attending the University of Alabama, he fell under the overpowering influence of Hubert Palmiller from a wealthy New York family. After Clarence's death while a missionary in Africa, Hubert married Lucinda Lankester, founded the Palmiller State Bank in Reedyville, produced two children, both named for Clarence—Clarry and Rance, whose tragedies stand at the heart of *The Looking-Glass* and whose fates link them with the Boutwells and the Nellohas at the opposite end of the social scale. After the death of her children Cindy, as she is known to Reedyville, divorced Hubert, who drifted back to a ne'er-do-well existence in New York. She married Robert Porterfield, the town's leading lawyer and her childhood sweetheart. Reedyville and the symbolized South thus keep unbroken the correct line of social prestige.

The Boutwells and the Nellohas, however, representing the poorwhite trash and foreigners, are the catalysts for breaking down some of the barriers of Reedyville's closed society. The Boutwells, who live on the edge of the town, are without doubt the most interesting and unusual family in the region. The father, the town handyman and drunk, is in his own mind a hero of the Spanish-American War; the mother is the special cleaning woman for the best homes on Reedy Avenue; the oldest daughter Fodie marries the town prostitute's son, Ira Graley, who later becomes a well-known psychologist; Stacy is a brakeman on the L & N; Dover ends up owning the town's leading garage built on Reedy Avenue on the very site of the Palmiller house; Breck in death becomes the town's World War I hero; and Honey makes a fortune in Paris night clubs and bistros as a singer of spirituals, where she is billed as *La Négresse d'Alabama.* Manny Nelloha's parents are the town junk dealers. He is spurred on to medical school by his consuming ambition and by a love-hate fixation for Clarry Palmiller. After his internship he returns to Reedyville under the assumed name of Dr. Snowfield. Tragic entanglements with Clarry as well as with Mattress Mae's ladies on New April Avenue finally force his departure from Alabama to revolutionary Russia.

It is, however, Breck Boutwell, the gay lover and poolroom owner, who by his memorial monument best illustrates the catalytic force for uniting and dividing the whole town, irrespective of address, money, or position. Though the incident of his monument is referred to in several stories and in *The Looking-Glass,* it is developed in full detail in "A Memorial to the Slain" (1945). The narrator is Mrs. Kent, the

doctor's wife, who sits on her comfortable front porch direct-
ing her cook Mamie in the preparation of turtle eggs given the
doctor by one of his patients "from up Pearl River way."

In 1920 when Reedyville, like many another town, discovers that it has no war memorial, the editor of the *Courier*
abetted by the Legion Post begins to work on public support.
Since Breck Boutwell is the only man of the town to be
killed in action, he is the obvious choice. A distinguished
committee with Robert Porterfield as chairman sets to work.
When Honey Boutwell hears of the matter—she has continued
to subscribe to the *Courier* during her career as Paris
chanteuse—she offers to contribute the remaining funds provided her friend Paul Gagnon is engaged to execute the
statue. After the Metropolitan Museum has verified Gagnon's
abilities, the committee accepts her offer.

The climax comes when the statue arrives entirely naked
and, in Mrs. Kent's words, "entirely complete." The original
plan called for placing the memorial in Courthouse Square,
but the committee after a private viewing decides that a background of greenery is needed, so Wentworth Park becomes
the site.

The advent of Breck in white marble divides the town into
three groups: Mr. Palmiller and his Society for the Fostering
of Temperance and the Eradication of Vice are determined to
have the offensive thing removed; Ella Doremus, the
librarian, is a spokesman for those who believe its artistic
value outweighs local prudery; the third group finds the
whole affair a grand joke with concurrent widespread
publicity for their business and their hometown.

The matter is finally resolved by militant action after the
girls from the canning factory have pronounced publicly and
often, "That's Breck Boutwell, all right . . . and no mistake."
Sister Joe Cotton, who appears in numerous Reedyville
stories, organizes a raid by the Vice Committee. They meet at
daybreak in front of Breck's statue. After a prayer and a
verse of "Stand Up, Stand Up for Jesus" Sister Cotton

"climbed on the pedestal, pulled a cold chisel out of her bosom and held it firmly while Mr. Palmiller swung his mallet and made Reedyville safe for both maidens and ladies already married." After this disfigurement Breck has to be removed for repairs to Moore's old livery stable, where no doubt he feels more at home.

In the background of the tragedies of *The Looking-Glass* or of the comedies like "Memorial to the Slain" solid middle-class citizens like Lillian Chapman from Tarleton's store go on with their everyday life. Lillian boosts the P.T.A. and goes with her husband on his annual furniture dealers' convention; Mrs. Kent rocks on her front porch ready to waylay the next passerby. Negroes like Lulu and Jesse, conscious of their menial roles, continue to humor their employers in whose peculiarities they take a certain public pride; but among themselves, particularly at numerous church functions, they give free vent to their more private thoughts.

Unlike Caldwell and Faulkner, March depicts his Reedyville with more attention to the *average* and the *daily* — the total fabric of the town. Reedyville has its Jeeter Lesters, its Compsons and Snopeses, but it has average Joes "upon the dull earth dwelling" who keep books, solicit freight, teach Sunday school, and sell shirts. Reedyville is the South, but it is also Everytown. Alistair Cooke has remarked:

> Small town life of the Deep South happens to be what [March] knows best, but Alabama is unlikely to crown him with laurel, for it becomes in his work a local habitation for many moods of the human spirit, and in his masterpiece, 'The Looking-Glass,' it is a microcosm of the universe. An Englishman, a Frenchman, or a Dane might in Reedyville recognize the spiritual anatomies of his neighbours, where Faulkner's famous county or Steinbeck's Cannery Row would only appall or fascinate him.

This shrewd observation by an Englishman is ironically underlined by the comments of contemporary American reviewers of March's work, who despite his many references to the geography and history of the state, seem to believe that the novels and stories take place "in the Delta country," "in Georgia," or in Faulkner's native state. Unwittingly they are admitting what Mr. Cooke has well observed: the actual locales are quite plainly drawn—a second reading will prove the point—but the spiritual and personal locales are so valid that the plantation, crossroads store, sawmill village, and county seat are where they are in each reader's unconscious geography. A writer of fiction can wish for no finer accolade.

The Alabama cities in March's fiction are treated somewhat differently. They are usually not the main settings for his stories, and when they are, these cities are sometimes generalized in a variety of methods. Birmingham is perhaps the most generalized of all. When Ruby Bogan, Bushrod Tarleton's debauched wife, deserts her long-suffering husband, she runs away with a Reedyville barber to live in Birmingham. Several incidents such as this seem to indicate that March views the large city as a dumping ground for the misfits and for those who desire to start life afresh.

Sometimes the cities are generalized as places of hotels, where the urban meet the rural, where acquaintances are purposefully or accidentally made or renewed. In *Company K* Private Leslie Jourdan recalls a very painful meeting with the concert pianist Henry Olsen, whom he has not seen since their student days in Paris in 1916. Henry cannot understand why Leslie has given up music until in desperation the latter displays his shrapnel-wrecked left hand. Then they talk of the successful paint business that Leslie is now operating in Birmingham. This terrifying, memorable incident occurs in "the lobby of the Tutweiler /sic/ Hotel."

It is in the lobby of the American Hotel in Montgomery that Joe Hinckley receives the first telegram about the approaching death of "the little wife." As he takes his seat on the train to Mobile, the heat waves shimmer above the hot slag roadbed and the muddy river that runs by the station.

Across from Joe on the red plush seat is a gaunt farm woman with a bunch of withered red crepe-myrtle. His unthinking words, "Lady, I hope you have a nice trip," merely remind her that she has been sent away from the city hospital because she waited too long for her goiter operation.

Montgomery and Birmingham are principally points of urban reference, but Mobile with its surrounding landscape is much more. This was of course the Alabama city best known to March: his place of birth and his manhood home when he was helping to found and expand the Waterman Steamship Lines and when he later retired to the South "to write as I please."

In his second novel, *Come In at the Door,* Mobile, where a portion of the story takes place, is called Bay City. On page 234, however, an oversight allows Miss Sarah Tarleton to write in her diary: "August 15, 1923. Spent a most pleasant week in Mobile with Bushrod and Chester." Whether March originally used Mobile in all references to the coastal city and merely failed to correct this one mention or whether this is a Freudian slip does not change the fact that the descriptions of the boarding house of the sailor Jim Saltis with its tattoo parlor on the first floor are vivid glimpses of the Alabama waterfront. Equally memorable is the description of the narrow brick house "decorated intricately with iron grille work" that Bushrod rented when Chester came to live permanently with him.

In his last novel, *The Bad Seed,* though the city is unnamed, the setting and total atmosphere unmistakably suggest the Mobile March knew.

In the center of the town, there was a square filled with azalea bushes, camellias and live oaks. There was a big, iron fountain with four graduated basins beneath to catch the cascading water from the top of the structure, to hold it a moment, and to pass it at least to the circular moat below. There was always a breeze at that place, and sometimes she'd take the child to the Square, knowing they'd not be likely to meet anyone but strangers in such a public place. They'd sit on the iron benches, while Christine looked vacantly about her, and Rhoda, on a separate bench, would go on with her needlework.

A more accurate description of Bienville Square would be hard to find, though it is the atmosphere rather than accuracy that here concerns the novelist. The apartment house that Christine and Rhoda Penmark have just left is also typical of many small-unit dwellings on Government Street and its side avenues.

The summer picnic grounds of the Fern School, where Rhoda as a student precipitates the drowning of little Claude Daigle, is typical of the old estates that formerly occupied sequestered spots along the Bay.

Mrs. Penmark parked at the Fern School gate, and Miss Octavia, spying her through the blinds, came down the walk to meet her. They rode for a time in silence, or discussing things in which neither had the least interest; and then, as they approached *Benedict,* and came down the long avenue of liveoaks and azaleas, Miss Fern said, 'You must examine our oleanders while you're here. They're very old. My grandfather planted them originally as a hedge to screen the place from the road, but now they're like trees. They're in full bloom at this season as you can see.'

An even better description of the area is written by Minnie McMinn, the Reedyville journalist in *The Looking-Glass,* after she had acquired a summer home there with the proceeds from her novels. She writes to Cindy Palmiller describing it:

Never, in all your life, have you seen anything so beautiful, Cindy . . . . My house is on top of a high cliff, and I like to think that the spot I live on is the place where the last Appalachian hill falls into the sea. I'm only a few hundred feet away from the little sandy beach below me; but between me and beach there is a thicket of pines, red gums, and magnolias, so that when I look down from the porch where I work [on *The Belle of Old*

Mobile], my lawn is the terraced tops of trees. In the morning I watch the sunrise below me in the east; in the afternoon I see it set in Mobile Bay. To the north of me is a network of rivers and bayous and lagoons; in front of me, shining through the trees, is the bay itself; to the south, on a clear day, I can see the Gulf of Mexico sparkling in the sun.

Even in his novel set in the South Pacific, *October Island,* March vividly recounts a strange Mobile episode about the sister of the heroine, Mrs. Barnfield. Having been paid $100,000 by the family of her husband to leave Philadelphia, Lurline buys a ticket to her old home, New Orleans.

But she was not destined to reach it, for when she was almost there the train stopped at a red-brick station beside a wide yellow river in which water hyacinths were drifting slowly toward the Gulf. Nearby, so close that she could hear the sound of its winches, a steamer was unloading bananas, and smelling the sweet, heavy scent, she stuck her head out of the coach window and asked the name of the town.

She was told that it was Mobile . . . .

And there she impulsively decides to spend the rest of her strange, miserly life.

Other Alabama cities find casual mention in March's fiction. They are, however, incidental and seem to be used to lend regional reality to his details. For example, when Fodie Boutwell finally divorces her brilliant, erratic husband, Ira Graley, she marries again, "this time quite happily. Her second husband was a Mr. Owen Witherspoon, and he was conventional, thrifty, cautious and respectable. They lived in Dothan, and she had acquired everything she wanted from life except, perhaps, a fountain with its three basins for her lawn." William March's Alabama is drawn against the urban background of Mobile and other cities from Dothan to Birmingham, but looming larger is the foreground of small towns and villages, plantations and farms.

7

Zelda Sayre Fitzgerald and Sara Haardt Mencken

IN 1917 when H.L. Mencken first cast a baleful eye on the South below the Potomac and found it a veritable "Sahara of the Bozart," Zelda Sayre was a senior at the Sidney Lanier High School in Montgomery, and Sara Haardt was a sophomore at Goucher College in Mencken's own Baltimore, having graduated a year earlier from the Margaret Booth School, a Montgomery seminary for young ladies. They were too young to react to Mencken's blast as did Emily Clark of Richmond: she solicited contributions and help from James Branch Cabell (the only Southern novelist Mencken considered of any consequence), Joseph Hergesheimer, and Mencken himself toward a projected literary journal to be known as the *Reviewer*. Both Zelda and Sara, however, without being aware of Mencken or his views about *Kultur* were themselves already reacting in other ways against the cloying scent of magnolias—the South they were to love and hate, flee from and return to, during their eventful lives.

Zelda, named for a gypsy queen from her mother's reading, was in open rebellion against genteel life in her small Southern city. According to Andrew Turnbull, biographer of Scott Fitzgerald, she called her father—State Supreme Court Judge Anthony Dickinson Sayre—"old Dick," dived off the highest crane at the gravel-pit swimming games, and delighted in riding behind a boy on a motorcycle at high speeds.

Montgomery, with a population of some 40,000 in 1917, was provincial and dull; she longed to be important and noticed in a world beyond her present confining one. A year later, in 1918, she began going out with soldiers from nearby Camp Sheridan; she smoked, sampled cocktails and made the rounds of country-club and college dances. Zelda was not, however, just another "fast" debutante. With cold logic re-enforced with soft Southern wiles, she was beginning to formulate what she later called a philosophy of flapperdom. "Youth does not need friends—it needs only crowds . . ." she wrote four years later; "I see no logical reasons for keeping the young illusioned . . . . They [should be] applying business methods to being young."

Sara Haardt, protesting against what she later called "this cloying, sickish, decadent land," had escaped as far as Baltimore with the financial aid of her maternal grandmother. In 1917—the year Mencken was writing the first version of his Southern "prejudices"—the death of her grandmother forced Sara to live more economically; she took a job as college postmistress to earn a little extra money. At Goucher she applied herself dilligently; in her first year she won the freshman short-story contest sponsored by the college literary magazine, *Kalends,* with her entry, "The Rattlesnake," and started working her way up to editor-in-chief of both *Kalends* and the college annual, *Donnybrook Fair.* During her summer vacation in 1919 as part in what her future husband called "a revolt against the thread-bare Confederate metaphysic," Sara headed the Alabama branch of the National Woman's Party and attempted vainly to persuade the Alabama Legislature to ratify the Nineteenth Amendment. Aided by some young Northern feminists, they "leaped to soap boxes," but only under the benign eye of Mayor William A. Gunter, who had known Sara from childhood.

Like Zelda, Sara "had danced assiduously in her time . . . undertaking what seems to have been a kind of ballet . . . before she came North"—the words are Mencken's; and Zelda in one of her first published magazine pieces in the June *Metropolitan* of 1922 is described in the editor's headnote as one not needing "to join the Lucy Stone League in order to identify herself as a personality. Everything Zelda Fitzgerald says and does stands out." Since recent biographers have recounted the career of Zelda Fitzgerald and in part that of Sara Mencken, a brief look at the strange way their lives intertwined, echoed, and contrasted with each other is appropriate, especially since they were friendly acquaintances rather than good friends in both Montgomery and Baltimore. With the exception of Sara Mayfield, who knew both women well, the principal biographers of the Fitzgeralds make no mention of Sara Mencken, and the biographers of Mencken make only brief references to Zelda Fitzgerald.

Sara Haardt and Zelda Sayre were both born in Montgomery, the former in 1898 and the latter in 1900, and both were educated in the schools of that city. Their families, at one time living within some seven blocks of each other, were conservative, upper middleclass, and Episcopalian. As children both were interested in Montgomery's version of ballet lessons. Turnbull records a hilarious account of Zelda's performance in the recital when she tripped on her skipping rope, entangling herself beyond hope and enjoying the whole fiasco more than the convulsed audience. As young ladies they were "rushed" by many of the same beaux, and they were "rebellious" in the spirit of the New South without being aware of such terms. Zelda's rebellion was social, Sara's intellectual and political; and both longed to see more of the world than the Black Belt towns of the Deep South.

As their dreams began to come true, the similarities of circumstance continued. Both were married to distinguished men of American letters: Zelda to F. Scott Fitzgerald in 1920 after a tempestuous World War I courtship, and Sara to

H.L. Mencken in 1930 after a quiet seven-year courtship—a marriage that caught the journalistic and literary worlds by surprise. With their husbands they traveled widely: the Fitzgeralds spent long periods during the 1920's in France and saw much of England and Italy; the Menckens honeymooned in Canada and later took a Caribbean and a Mediterranean cruise, including a trip to the Holy Land. Both traveled extensively in the United States, the Fitzgeralds living by turns in New York, Connecticut, Minnesota, Delaware, Maryland, and Alabama. In January, 1927, they also paid a two-months' visit to Hollywood. Fitzgerald needed cash, was curious about his abilities as a scriptwriter, and had accepted a contract from United Artists to do a screen story for Constance Talmadge. Zelda found Hollywood at first exciting but later rather flashily dull. Accordingly, she and Scott enlivened it with pranks of their own. Once, it is reported, they appeared at a party in nightgown and pajamas, parodying actors' habits of dressing in the costumes they wore on their current sets. Later in 1927, after the Fitzgeralds had returned to Wilmington, Sara Haardt spent five months in Hollywood under a contract to Famous Players. Mencken wrote his good friend Jim Tully that Sara "is in Hollywood simply because the Jews offered her a chance to get some easy money." According to Carl Bode's *Mencken,* Sara collected fifteen hundred dollars for her script, "The Promise Land," an unproduced film about Confederate refugees in Brazil.

In addition to her interest in Fitzgerald's fiction and her helpful criticism that he often acknowledged, Zelda wrote on her own. For *College Humor* she did a series of pieces that she told Henry Dan Piper were merely "potboilers written to pay for her ballet lessons." Of particular interest is "Southern Girl," Zelda's version of the same material Fitzgerald used in "The Ice Palace." She also wrote a number of essays and short stories, some done jointly with Scott and some on her own, as well as her novel, *Save Me the Waltz* (1932). Besides her serious interest and hard work in the ballet in this country and in Paris, Zelda painted with considerable ability; *Time* reviewed one of her exhibitions in Cary Ross's Manhattan studio. Early in her career, Sara Haardt also did some pieces for *College Humor* as well as serious literary criticism for journals like the *Bookman, North American Review,* and the Richmond *Reviewer.* She wrote many essays (particularly about Alabama and the South) for *Country Life, Scribner's,* and the *American Mercury;* about forty short stories, seventeen of which Mencken gathered in the posthumous collection *Southern Album* (1936), and a novel, *The Making of a Lady* (1931)—an earlier novel "Career" having failed to find a publisher.

Both Zelda and Sara were strikingly beautiful as young girls and young women. Zelda had, according to Edmund Wilson, red-gold hair and an astonishing prettiness. As she grew older her hair became a glossy dark gold that Fitzgerald compared to a chow's; the upper part of her face was chiseled and almost hawklike with firm brow and nose and remarkable gray-blue eyes that turned black with excitement. Despite her sometimes hoydenish ways she had an innate grace and dignity of movement. Sara, like Zelda, was rather tall, with soft brown hair and eyes, and according to Mencken's biographer, William Manchester, "a delicate frame [of] Camelialike beauty." Mencken urged her for her health's sake to gain weight, and once he announced solemnly that he was planning to be accompanied on a journey by his wife, a buxom German soprano. She had a kind of shy good humor and an easy laugh. Gladys Baker of the Birmingham *News,* who happened to interview her about the time of her marriage, found her to be the epitome of a southern lady. Many commentators have spoken of the warm southern voices of these two women that never changed despite their cosmopolitan lives, and Mencken summed up his wife's memory "under the banal name of Southern charm" with an accent "that left her r's soft and thin as gossamer."

Finally, Sara and Zelda were afflicted with diseases that ended in sudden and tragic deaths. Zelda's struggle with schizophrenia is well known, though Miss Mayfield in *Exiles from Paradise* believes that Dr. Adolph Meyer's opinion of the Fitzgeralds as a dual case, *folie à deux,* is the better diagnosis. From at least 1927 Zelda was beset with disturbing manifestations and from 1930 to her death was in and out of mental institutions in Europe and in this country. In her last years she moved between the Highland Hospital (for mental and nervous diseases) in Asheville, North Carolina, and her mother's home in Montgomery; sometimes, according to Turnbull, walking "[its] streets in a long black dress and a floppy hat with an open Bible before her and her lips moving." Sara was the victim of tuberculosis, having spent parts of 1924 and 1925 in a Maryland sanitarium. She recovered from two serious operations in 1928 and 1929, spent almost half of her married life in and out of hospitals and doctors' care, and died suddenly of meningitis and tubercular infection of the spine in 1935. Zelda was the tragic victim of a fire in 1948 that swept one building of the Highland Hospital.

These similarities in the lives of Zelda Sayre and Sara Haardt, however, should not obscure the marked contrasts in their characters. The two years' difference in their ages and their attendance at different schools in Montgomery did not encourage close friendship, and, while Zelda was being the belle of many balls in Alabama and Georgia and being courted by Scott Fitzgerald, Sara was away at Goucher. Later, when the Fitzgeralds moved to Baltimore in 1932 so that Zelda might have psychiatric treatment at Johns Hopkins, the couples apparently saw something of each other; but, according to Manchester, "after one trying evening at Rodgers Forge [the Turnbulls' estate], Mencken forbade Sara to have anything more to do with them [the Fitzgeralds]." Mencken, it must be remembered, believed, like Hemingway, that Zelda was destroying her husband;

Mencken's close friend and associate, Charles Angoff, reports him as remarking once after a painful visit to Fitzgerald's hotel suite, "Scott will never amount to a hoot in hell till he gets rid of his wife." Yet Sara Mayfield, an Alabama friend of both Zelda and Sara, records in *The Constant Circle* that when she and Sara Haardt first met Mencken, he said of Zelda, " 'What a girl! Cleverer than Scott, if the truth were known. I've no doubt but that she startled the booboisie in the Bible Belt' "; and to me Miss Mayfield commented about the Baltimore period that Mencken's attitude toward the Fitzgeralds

> was not precipitated by any one incident but was the result of many misadventures, including the disastrous visit of Scott and Zelda to the Hergesheimers. At the time that Mencken issued his ukase to both Sara and me, Zelda was in the hospital, Scott was at a loose end and being both difficult and tedious. Mr. Mencken, however, was motivated solely by his desire to protect us from any of the unpleasantness that Scott was continually being involved in and not by any personal animus. And, he himself continued to be courteous and friendly to Scott as long as he lived.

In Forgue's edition of the selected letters, Mencken always remembers during these years to ask "Fitz" about Zelda and to express his hope that she is improving. Miss Mayfield summed up to me her impression of the relationship: " . . . the real friendship . . . when the Fitzgeralds were living in Baltimore [was] between Sara and Zelda, rather than between them [the Menckens] and Scott, where the relation was more literary than personal." Although Turnbull does not mention Sara Haardt in his *Scott Fitzgerald*, his comment in a letter to me is similar to Miss Mayfield's: "I don't believe the Fitzgeralds and the Menckens were ever intimate, not even in the Twenties (Fitzgerald was a little in awe of Mencken), and in the Thirties their relations were formal." In *The Constant Circle* Miss Mayfield says that in 1933 when

Fitzgerald lived in a modest apartment near the Menckens, "he often arrived unannounced at odd hours, often with strange companions picked up on the streets." Since the Menckens' own domestic life was ordered and decorous, Mencken himself "had little patience with the chronic disorder in the life of Fitzgerald."

Despite their Montgomery background and later proximity in Baltimore, where they saw something of each other, Zelda Sayre and Sara Haardt were quite different personalities. Many witnesses have recorded Zelda's "show-off antics," from the time as a child when she called the Montgomery fire department to rescue the Sayres' little girl and obligingly climbed out on the roof so the men would have someone to rescue, to the time when at a party she presented her lace panties as a farewell gift to Alexander Woollcott. Because, according to many observers, she always maintained a kind of sweet dignity throughout these exhibitionist escapades and usually seemed to be performing more for herself than for others, her personality is enigmatic. Ernest Hemingway and Rebecca West said bluntly well before 1927 that Zelda was insane. In sharp contrast Sara Haardt always impressed people as being quiet, retiring—a brunette foil to the blonde Zelda. When Mencken, who had known Sara for several years in Baltimore as teacher, writer, and doctoral student in psychology, heard that she was going to Hollywood, he wrote Jim Tully, who was living there at the time:

> Miss Haardt, of whom I wrote you sometime ago, left for Hollywood yesterday, I hope you will find it possible to see her. She was brought up in Montgomery, Alabama, and is still extremely shy. The life in Hollywood will probably shock her half to death. I think you'll like her very much. She is immensely amiable. Moreover, she has a great deal of talent.

Sara Haardt was a hard-working college student at Goucher from 1916 to 1920 and a teacher at her Montgomery alma mater, the Margaret Booth School, from 1920 to 1922, after which she returned to Goucher as one of the youngest members ever to serve on its faculty. A Phi Beta Kappa student, she had disciplined herself to an orderly life in the literary circle of Emily Clark, James Branch Cabell, Joseph Hergesheimer, and H.L. Mencken. During these same years Zelda Sayre was married to the most glamorous novelist in America, and she and Scott Fitzgerald savored life expensively in and around New York, the French Riviera, and Paris.

Zelda at twenty married a young man who shared most of her tastes and cravings for the glitter of what he later called the Jazz Age. At twenty-four Fitzgerald was immensely ambitious, and had just sold his first novel to Scribner's; he looked up worshipfully to H.L. Mencken as the most dynamic critic of American life and letters. Sara Haardt, with some considerable formal education and solid literary accomplishment behind her, married the Sage of Baltimore, who in 1930 was fifty and had begun to concern himself with linguistic, political, and philosophic fields rather than with criticism of imaginative literature. In short, Sara was for Henry Mencken a "violet" from the "Sahara of the Bozart"—actually one of her first published pieces was a poem in the *Bookman* called "White Violets"—while Zelda was for Scott Fitzgerald "a barbarian princess" from the South, "of dreamy skies and firefly evenings."

Aside from schoolroom assignments Zelda Sayre probably did her first serious writing in her diary and in her long letters to Scott Fitzgerald between 1918 and 1920. She let him read her diary, and in his drab room in the Bronx, when he was working in New York, he said that his "fixation [was] upon the day's letter from Alabama." Parts of her diary and passages from her letters, like the well-known one about the Confederate cemetery, were eventually used in *This Side of Paradise* and *The Beautiful and Damned;* and according to Arthur Mizener, these extracts were "like all she

wrote . . . brilliant amateur work." Her oral compositions—
her conversations—were also a stimulus to Fitzgerald. He says
in "Early Success" that he began to change from an amateur
to a professional writer when he had finished his first novel
and was waiting for Scribner's to publish it: "I had been an
amateur before; in October [actually November, 1919],
when I strolled with a girl among the ruins of a southern
graveyard, I was a professional and my enchantment with
certain things that she felt and said was already paced by an
anxiety to set them down in a story—it was called *The Ice
Palace.*" And after he had written the story, Zelda replied,
"It's so nice to know you really *can* do things—anything—and
I love to feel that maybe I can help just a little."

But in 1922, half serious and half in jest, Zelda was quoted
in the New York *Tribune* about *The Beautiful and Damned:*
"It seems to me that on one page I recognize a portion of an
old diary of mine which mysteriously disappeared shortly
after my marriage, and also scraps of letters which, though
considerably edited, sound to me vaguely familiar. In fact,
Mr. Fitzgerald—I believe that is how he spells his name—
seems to believe that plagiarism begins at home." This desire
to compete led her to devote energy to writing just as she did
later to dancing and painting when they became almost
manias with her. Fitzgerald's friends were disturbed by this
strange partnership. Hemingway, for example, wrote to
Fitzgerald: "Of all people on earth you need discipline in
your work and instead you marry someone who is jealous of
your work, wants to compete with you and ruins you . . . and
you complicate it even more by being in love with her."
Fitzgerald himself was ambivalent in his attitude toward his
wife's writing. At times they worked on pieces together, like
those in *Esquire,* "Show Mr. and Mrs. F. to Number——" and
"Auction—Model 1934": "Zelda and I collaborated [he
wrote Maxwell Perkins]—idea, editing, and padding being
mine and most of the writing being hers." Or as Turnbull
describes the same collaboration: "It was a grim year [1934]

for Fitzgerald . . . . [He] rewrote three articles of Zelda's for *Esquire."* "The Millionaire's Girl," however, was published under the name of F. Scott Fitzgerald. According to Mizener, Harold Ober, their literary agent, tried to correct the mistake, but the *Saturday Evening Post* presses had already started to roll. Turnbull calls it "a story she wrote"; Mizner refers to it as "wholly . . . by Zelda," but later when he lists Fitzgerald's published works he labels it "largely written by Zelda"; Piper in his updated "Check List" classified it "mostly written by Zelda." And Zelda herself has complicated the matter even further by remarking to James Montgomery Flagg that she signed Scott's name to pieces she had written so that she could get better prices for them. Even in a story like "The Millionaire's Girl," then, where the style and subject matter are Zelda's, the circumstances of authorship are not clear.

Sometimes Fitzgerald appears almost annoyed with Zelda's ability as a writer. He wrote one of her psychiatrists: ". . . unless a story comes to her fully developed and crying to be told she's liable to flounder around rather unsuccessfully among problems of construction"; and in a letter to Dr. Murdock: ". . . my writing was more important than hers by a large margin, because of the years of preparation for it, and the professional experience, and because my writing kept the mare going."

Fitzgerald's varying attitudes must always be interpreted against the background of Zelda's writing as therapy as well as against that of his own seeming jealousy. Whatever the case—and it varied over the years—the problem of discovering what besides *Save Me the Waltz* Zelda actually wrote is not an easy one. Piper summarizes his bibliographic studies of the Fitzgeralds: "It is difficult to determine precisely just how much of the writing in [certain] items should be credited to each of them." Here it will be sufficient to examine representative pieces generally acknowledged to be Zelda's.

Like Scott Fitzgerald she was a commentator on the Jazz Age; one of her articles for the *Metropolitan* examines the

1922 status of the flapper. Zelda declares that the flapper is now deceased, her accoutrements having been bequeathed to girls' schools, debutantes, and big-town shop-girls. Flapperdom, which has become a game, was originally "a philosophy."

The flapper awoke from her lethargy of subdebism, bobbed her hair, put on her choicest pair of earrings and a great deal of audacity and rouge and went into battle. She flirted because it was fun to flirt and wore a one-piece bathing suit because she had a good figure, she covered her face with powder and paint because she didn't need it and she refused to be bored chiefly because she wasn't boring.

Although the brief essay may be an apologia *pro prima vita sua*, it is sparkling, pointed, and intended to shock.

Also like her husband Zelda uses the background of her own life and emotions for much of her shorter fiction. In "The Millionaire's Girl" the glamor of Hollywood furnishes the backdrop for the story of Caroline, who is determined "to distinguish herself and force Barry to realize the enormity of his error in leaving her." After paying a visit to the "Fitzgerald's roadhouse" in Westport, Caroline goes to Hollywood, and with "her beautiful Biblical eyes" she becomes a star. But the premiere of her movie is hollow because she reads of Barry and his new fiancée in Paris; during the premiere Caroline is sped past the Hollywood movie house in an ambulance, an attempted suicide. Barry rushes to her side, but the narrator comments on their possible reconciliation: "I am a cynical person, no competent judge of idyllic young love affairs."

Similarly "A Couple of Nuts" reflects the Fitzgeralds' days in France with the Gerald Murphys, the same material that Scott was using in *Tender Is the Night* and Zelda in parts of *Save Me the Waltz*. Larry and Lola are a couple of American nightclub singers, when "the summer of 1924 shrivelled the trees in the Champs Elysées." They are violently in love with each other and yet they drink and quarrel as violently. Lola, who has "hunter's eyes that trapped and slew her mouth," has an affair with Jeff Daugherty, a rich American émigré, and Larry has his affair with Jeff's ex-wife Mabel. He is drowned on her yachting party, but Lola goes on begging money from friends like the narrator, who believes that the singer will last a while longer, since "it takes a good thirty years to batter down a woman's looks and crumple the charm she acquires from moving in a world she finds rich . . . ." Lola was still "one of the few women . . . who was both fluffy enough and concise enough to be pretty in ermine." But no more will she come home to Larry "after break-fast . . . ska[ting] in on his eggs, so to speak." Professor Piper is right in referring to Zelda's as a "talent that comes through to us in her remarkable synesthetic prose."

During Zelda's first mental breakdown in Europe she produced, according to Mizener, a libretto for a ballet and several short stories: "Miss Bessie," "A Workman," "The Drouth and the Flood," and "The House." When *Scribner's Magazine* rejected the last three, which Turnbull describes as "subsequently lost," Fitzgerald urged Maxwell Perkins to make a book out of them along with the sketches "that attracted so much attention in *College Humor.*" The scheme came to naught, but *Scribner's* later published "Miss Bessie" under the title "Miss Ella" in its December issue of 1931. It is a story full of the lush descriptions and melodramatic events that Zelda liked. The atmosphere and setting is the Deep South, and the narrative is told from a not-quite-realized point of view of a child who remembers climbing over Miss Ella's garden wall and being warned away from the steps of the old playhouse, where one of Miss Ella's suitors had shot his brains out on the day of her proposed wedding to another. Now Miss Ella's life is primarily confined to her hammock in the garden where "the southern spring passed, the violets and the yellow white pear trees and the jonquils and cape jasmine gave up their tenderness to the deep green lullaby of early May."

Also like Scott, Zelda, wrote a play, *Scandalabra,* which the Vagabond Players produced in Baltimore in the spring of 1933. It was even less successful than his earlier drama, *The Vegetable, or from President to Postman.* In the medium of letter writing, though, Zelda has few peers—at least from the samples that are now available. To Maxwell Perkins Zelda described Scott's preparation to speak to a liberal group at Johns Hopkins about his "old twenties feeling about war." Mizener quotes the following extract:

> The community Communist comes and tells us about a kind of Luna Park Eutopia . . . . I have taken somewhat eccentrically at my age, to horseback riding which I do as non-commitally as possible so as not to annoy the horse. Also very apologetically since we've had so much communism lately that I'm not sure it's not the horse who should be riding me.

In the earlier desperate days of their courtship by mail Zelda wrote Scott with what is surely a charmingly mature wit for a girl of nineteen: "That first abandon couldn't last, but the things that went to make it are tremendously alive . . . . I know you've worried—and enjoyed it thoroughly . . . you're so morbidly exaggerative . . . . Sort of deliberately experimental and wiggly." Frequently her later letters to "Dearest Scott" written from hospitals recall their days in Alabama: "The wall was damp and mossy when we crossed the street and said we loved the south. I thought of the south and a happy past I'd never had and I thought I was part of the south. The wisteria along the fence was green and the shade was cool and life was old." Even in her disturbed state, writes Turnbull, "she wrote a letter better than most people are capable of in their right minds." An edition of her letters is needed.

Save Me the Waltz is without doubt Zelda's best work. Begun in Montgomery in 1931 under the influence of her father's last illness and Scott's absence in Hollywood, it was finished in the quiet of Phipps Clinic in Baltimore after her second breakdown. The novel is her autobiographic testament, more accurate in detail than Mizener hints when he cites the exactness of hotel room numbers and photographic snapshots: it contains accurate statements about family background—senators and Confederate generals—impressions of Montgomery, the Riviera, Paris, and Naples, and most important of all, Zelda's view of herself—her girlhood, her marriage, and her struggle against boredom. One of Zelda's sisters commented to me: "The figures in her story whom I knew are drawn with keen perception, particularly those of our parents. (To be with them again I have only to read the book.)" Whatever may be true of the novel, it is neither "contrived" nor "tedious" as Professor Hoffman labels it in a footnote to *The Twenties;* nor does it "fail" as Professor Piper maintains, because "it rarely arouses any emotion except pity." *Save Me the Waltz* is eminently readable, and its theme has become more valid with the passing years.

As a first novel, however, it has many weaknesses. The *Saturday Review* suggested that there was too frequent "strained metaphor." But this stylistic device is usually confined to the beginnings of chapters and reserved for descriptions of geography and the passage of time: at the opening of the last chapter set in Montgomery, she writes: "The David Knights stepped out of the old brick station. The Southern town slept soundless on the wide palette of the cotton-fields." The language, particularly in the first half of the story, is riotous and *précieuse;* in their Connecticut home, "playing about the room in the lalique ten o'clock sun, they were like two uncombed sealyhams." At other times the language borders on Imagist prose poetry: in the hot Alabama summer "they hired a buggy and drove through the dust to daisy fields like nursery rhymes where dreamy cows saddled with shade nibbled the summer off the white slopes." Almost all the reviewers commented on the lack of proof-reading, particularly in French words and names of musicians, but this fault may be laid, in part at least, at the door of Maxwell Perkins and Scribner's, who were accustomed to coping with the notorious misspellings of Fitzgerald himself. It is also true that certain narrative links occasionally seem to be omitted—Bonnie is born, then she talks, and only later do we discover that she was two years old at that time. Though this technique annoyed Fitzgerald, who always prefers sharp outlines of narration, he pointed out in its defense to Perkins that "the form of so many modern novels is less a progression than a series of impressions, as you know." The most disturbing element in the book is the somewhat shadowy character of David Knight, the young artist who experiences meteoric fame after World War I and marries Alabama Beggs. The second section, however, which is the logical spot for the unfolding of David's character and motivations, is the weakest in the novel. This is the part set on the Riviera that in its original form infuriated Scott when he first read it because it dealt with a portrait of himself, then called Amory Blaine after his own collegiate hero in *This Side of Paradise*—material he was using in his own next novel. Perkins and Fitzgerald together persuaded Zelda to rewrite this section, and as such it probably suffers in relation to the whole story.

If Fitzgerald is petulantly responsible for weakening the middle part of the book and thereby fuzzing his own fictional portrait, he can perhaps claim some credit for the admirable balanced plotting of the work in four sections, each with three chapters, ending where it begins in Montgomery. The strength of the novel, unlike many first novels, lies primarily in its characters. The reader *cares* about Alabama Knight and her struggles against great odds to be a ballerina. The musty, dusty Paris studio seven flights up with its extreme heat in summer and cold in winter, its jealous, temperamental students—all mysteriously and understandingly presided over by Madame—is the setting for the climax of the story. David feels neglected by Alabama's continuous presence in the studio and her eternal practice at home. And their daughter Bonnie, who has what Alabama did not have— a chance to start ballet young—is only superficially interested in it. Surrounded by nannies and governesses she is at once a charming, imaginative, and snobbish little child, whose fictional portrait is to be continued in Fitzgerald's "Babylon Revisited." Many of the minor characters are also well portrayed: Alabama's mother Millie, who sews tirelessly for her children, smooths out the Judge's world, and raises three daughters to be other men's wives, is an appealing portrait of the Southern gentlewoman of the generation after the Civil War. And Judge Beggs himself typifies the dominant parent who is an equitable tower of moral strength—a literary forebear of Harper Lee's Atticus Finch in *To Kill a Mockingbird.*

The theme of *Save Me the Waltz* is perennially valid for the twentieth century: the development of the full potential of the talented woman who marries young and fails to find satisfaction in domestic pursuits. She must cope with the memory of a subservient mother, the inevitable dominance and pull of a husband and child, as well as the encroachment of age. At the same time she desires to hold together the past and present family circles. The small degree of triumph that comes to Alabama Knight in the ballet of the San Carlos Opera in Naples also could have some to Zelda herself, according to Nancy Milford's *Zelda;* but "inexplicably she did not take" her San Carlos offer. The breakdown of the body is often reparable; the breakdown of the mind is sometimes irreparable. Although there is much about the Fitzgeralds to be learned from *Save Me the Waltz* as a study in therapeutic autobiography, as a novel it stands on its own; it deserves another reading.

Despite its lack of consistency of stylistic tone and its attitudinal point of view, it is a moving story that sweeps along with the rhythm of its waltz. The title, borrowed from a Victor record catalogue, is a magic stroke, for it suggests the central struggle of the dance, the glamor of the waltzing world of Connecticut, Paris, and St. Raphael of the 1920's, as well as the romantic, enduring love that hero and heroine have for each other.

As Zelda grew older and her interest in Biblical images and diction increased along with her mental illness, she planned and executed a 135-page MS of a novel called "Caesar's Things" about "the Biblical pattern of life [in] its everyday manifestations." According to Mrs. Milford, the same characters and much of the same autobiographical material of *Save Me the Waltz* is retold—this time with visitations from God and with an increasingly incoherent piling of image on image. One wonders (if he could have seen it) what Mencken would have thought about this work from the clever girl who shocked "the booboisie in the Bible Belt."

There is, on the contrary, little difficulty in determining the bibliography of Sara Haardt's works. When she married Mencken in 1930, she was a well-established free-lance writer, and during her married years she continued to write and publish under the name of Sara Haardt. In fact, during the great Depression when Mencken's own books, like those of most writers, were selling slowly and the *American Mercury* was falling on hard times, he took especial joking pride in Sara's writing. In a letter to Philip Goodman in 1933 he remarks: "Sara, whose chief market is the woman's magazines, sold more stuff within the last month than she had ever sold before in a whole year. Moreover, she is beset with orders. Thus I hope that she'll earn enough by 1934 to support me in reasonable decency." His serious attitude was the opposite of Fitzgerald's toward Zelda's writing. Mencken rejoiced in Sara's every success.

The Menckens had carefully arranged their lives so that they would not disturb each other's work habits. They breakfasted separately and each had a private study. At four-thirty each afternoon they met in what Mencken called the "public rooms" for discussion before dinner, and frequently there were guests for either lunch or dinner. Between the two there was little literary collaboration; their interests were quite different. Before their marriage, however, Sara had done a long, tedious job for Mencken in going through his thirty-odd volumes of newspaper clippings to prepare *Menckeniani: a Schimpflexikon*—a task he duly acknowledges in his memorial preface to her posthumous *Southern Album*. She also assisted with editing the *American Mercury* and undertook other research jobs like the immense dossier on the Civil War she prepared for Joseph Hergesheimer when he was planning *Swords and Roses*.

Aside from her novel, research work for other writers, and the Monday column in the *Sun* (which Mencken wrote for the other weekdays), Sara Haardt's work can be grouped into three major categories: literary criticism and book reviews, essays and articles chiefly about the South, and short stories. The two most interesting contributions to the first category are her pieces in the 1929 *Bookman* on Ellen Glasgow and Hergesheimer, both of whom she admired as friends and as writers. The article on Miss Glasgow uses her gray stone house in Richmond and its comfortable upstairs study, with the collections of Staffordshire and Chelsea dogs, as a background for comments on the author's life and writing. Believing that "the South has seldom been aware of its writers and, almost never, influenced by them," Miss Haardt traces the life of Ellen Glasgow and demonstrates how this prim, pretty, outwardly conforming woman was actually, despite her polished style, the first of the Southern *révoltés* from a genteelism to a new realism in depicting the tragic lot of the gentlewoman in the Victorian South—an era "above all . . . of waiting." Now, in 1929, Miss Glasgow is ironically the defender of the traditions of the Old South. "The only art that has ever succeeded in the South," says Miss Glasgow, "is the art of hypocrisy."

The essay, "Joseph Hergesheimer's Methods," is written in like manner, against the background of Hergesheimer's beautifully restored Dower House in Pennsylvania. Miss Haardt describes in detail Hergesheimer's methods of saturating himself with historical documents for such works as *Quiet Cities* and *Swords and Roses:* the vast energy of the manner of his preparation and concern with just the right bit of symbolic scenery or incident in the lives of his men, women, or cities to use as a focal point for the entire essay. After Hergesheimer had absorbed hundreds of books, dossiers of information by assistants, he would write steadily at a clip of three thousand words a day. It seems quite probable that Hergesheimer's fascination with historical and realistic background influenced Sara Haardt in the methods of her own writing. Certainly in many essays, like "Southern Credo" and "Alabama," she captures much of the same verve. In *The Making of a Lady,* however, this method of vivid background allied with impressionistic "overheard" conversations from people on sidewalks or front porches often splinters attention from the central story.

In the second category—essays and articles chiefly about the South—Sara wrote a series of pieces about antiques for *Country Life:* "Glass Bells of Days Gone By," "Love Letters of Long Ago," and "Shells of Fond Memory." She herself was an avid purchaser of Victorian bric-a-brac, having assembled so many collections of glass bells, quaint Valentines, and old-fashioned china pin-boxes and shellwork pictures that Mencken had to leave his assemblage of cuckoo clocks in Hollins Street. Her more serious essays, however, concerned the South. Early in her career she had written pleasant, piquant little sketches of Southern characters for Emily Clark's Richmond *Reviewer,* but her more recent work dealt with the dichotomy of an old South of magnolia blossoms and memories and a new South of factories and pellagra. The pattern for most of these essays is a series of contrasting narratives that form an expository whole. In her "Alabama," for example, published in the *American Mercury* in 1925, the first section, "Here We Rest," points out that although the linguistic scholars have long ago agreed that

Alabama does not mean "here we rest," but something like "vegetation gatherers" or "thicket clearers," Alabamians go right on teaching and believing the former figment of A.B. Meek's romantic imagination. The second section, "Industrial Note," cites evidence of the economic booms of old cities like Florence, Huntsville, and Tuscaloosa. The third section, "Anniversaries," narrates the contrasting celebrations of the quiet centenary of Lafayette's famous visit to the state as compared with the bustling Epworth League Ladies' rally for the Fifth Birthday of the Eighteenth Amendment. In sharper contrast, the fourth section, "Paradise Regained," recounts how in this dry state one can charmingly acquire any amount or variety of scuppernong, dewberry, dandelion, elderberry wines or peach, blackberry, or tomato cordials from most any rural neighborhood, especially when the season for church bazaars is at hand. And thus the essay proceeds for ten sections, which ultimately form the ironic facets of the state that doubtless delighted the heart of the *Mercury's* editor, H.L. Mencken, as well as anticipated by some years the pattern of Carl Carmer's *Stars Fell on Alabama.*

Another essay that follows the same plan is "Southern Credo" of 1930; here Miss Haardt relates one of her favorite incidents, which she latter uses in both short story and novel, about General Pickett's not leading Pickett's famous charge at Gettysburg, but instead remaining behind a barn. Though old Captain Faulkner, who entertained the author as a child sitting on the Capitol portico near Jefferson Davis' gold star, knows these facts about Pickett, he will not acknowledge them. "How like the South that is—how irreconciliable! . . . Pickett will continue to receive the glory." Though Sara could objectively recount these ironic incidents, she herself was part of the "credo," as Mencken delightedly recalls on seeing her put aside Freeman's *Lee* because certain portions of the biography made Lee seem silly and she could never bear to think of Lee as silly.

In "Southern Town," published in the *North American Review* of 1931, she continues to draw pointed sketches that illustrate the divisive nature of the South, and in "The Etiquette of Slavery," written in 1929 for the *American Mercury,* she presents numerous incidents from fact and fiction to support the thesis that "unfortunately, these rules [of etiquette], though they . . . had the purpose of making the institution [of slavery] tolerable, often only made master and mistress the slaves of their slaves." Her style in these essays is pleasant and competent, and her material is usually fresh because it is nearly always based on her personal knowledge and informed experience, like "Are Doctors People?" written for *Hygeia* in 1934.

The third category—the short story—is best represented by the collection, *Southern Album,* which Mencken edited after his wife's death, though two of her best or most typical stories are omitted. One is "Licked," which was her first piece of fiction in the *American Mercury* of September, 1927. Like Eugene O'Neill's *The Straw,* it depicts a tuberculosis sanitarium with its small world of gossip, hope, fear, and death. It does not resort to emotional melodrama, and it is not spoiled by neat turns of events as her later story, "The Manor," is somewhat spoiled when the fall of the elevator in the genteel hotel for old ladies precipitates the inevitable death of Lucinda Vaughn. In "Licked" the mood of the story is allowed to dominate, but in "The Manor" the carefully wrought atmosphere is almost dissipated by chance happenings. The second story omitted from Mencken's edition is "Absolutely Perfect," which was reprinted from the *Woman's Home Companion* in the *O. Henry Prize Stories* of 1933. Olive Wylie, who lives in the static little town of Verbena, Alabama, disobeys her mother and goes to her first country club dance with her college beau, Russ Cobb, from Birmingham. She finds the older crowd not very good dancers, and although Russ invites her up to the Phoenix Club for next

Saturday night, she regrets leaving her high school set. Even though her mother has now relented and given her permission to attend club dances, Olive realizes that she irretrievably stepped over the line into adulthood and that there is not even a mother to whom she can now retreat and acknowledge her error.

Of the seven stories in *Southern Album* on this same theme of a girl's awareness of the borders of childhood, none is better than "Absolutely Perfect." Mencken, who rather liked stories about little girls, just as he was always charmed by all small children whom he treated quite seriously, admits that his selection of seventeen stories for *Southern Album* might not have been Sara's. But the volume has a certain unity in its world of the Southern woman from childhood to old age, and while the style and method of telling is never unusual or arresting, it is smooth and workmanlike.

The two best stories are "Miss Rebecca" and "Dear Life." The former is a study of the "silver cord" theme of a mother who even in old age will not release her daughter—a mother with the vicious habit of playing up to Rebecca's suitors to their faces but ridiculing them behind their backs. Old Mrs. Simpson is given to making remarks like "The oldest Sayre girl has announced her engagement to that young man who used to come here . . . you remember . . . he had quite a time with his meat at your party." In "Dear Life," which Mencken considers "hardly fiction," Sara does her best job of a story of tone and atmosphere that gradually reveals the narrator's attitude toward her native South. "Full of her [Sara's] private feelings and reflections," according to Mencken, the story runs a gamut of recollections about the past and of reactions to the present hospital experiences of the narrator, who concludes:

> If I had thought I was escaping death when I escaped with my life—my dear life!—from the hospital, then I was as pretty a fool as when I thought I was escaping death in escaping the South. I

had come back to sit at my own wake .... My heart had gone
out in reconciliation to the South at last.

As William Rose Benét remarked in the *Saturday Review,*
"Miss Haardt seems to have known her South in a period of
change."

Of her novel *The Making of a Lady* comment is difficult.
The idea of a young heroíne, handicapped by a sloppy, white-
trashy mother and by a poor address, who succeeds in
marrying the son of General Haviland, Meridian's wealthiest
and most respected citizen, is a good subject for a novel. And
Beulah Miller is a worthy literary descendant of Augusta
Evans Wilson's Beulah Hartwell, who in *Beulah* (1850) pre-
vails against all the speculative philosophers because she is
fortified with a Methodist faith. A part of the book's failure,
as the *New York Times* indicated, is the author's inability to
"create character." The transcriptions of the overheard conversations are authentic, and the struggles for social and
economic position are valid; but, as the *Saturday Review*
found, the novel "lacks not continuity, but continuousness.
There are gaps in the story and gaps in the characters. There
are, however, no gaps in Meridian the town." Meridian is Miss
Haardt's name for a sleepy Montgomery from the turn of the
century to the awakening, hectic days of World War I with its
army camps and booming syrup factories and fertilizer
plants. A vivid account of the kind of town in which Sara
Haardt and Zelda Sayre grew up, it is somehow too full of
details after the manner of Mencken's favorite novelist,
Dreiser; the canvas lacks perspective and what painters once
called a vanishing point. It is almost as if Miss Haardt wanted
to say everything that she had said in her essays and short
stories over again: the rosewood piano with the Yankee
bullet lodged in it, penny-poppy shows and four-o'clock and
daisy chains, Confederate cemeteries, the pettiness of girls'
schools, the influential power of Negro nurses—all of these
are repeated here. A structural flaw that makes the novel

seem even more scattered is the point of view in the telling. Sometimes life is seen through Beulah's eyes, and sometimes the story seems to unfold in vague omniscience.

Sara Haardt, according to Mencken, was well aware of the faults of this novel, even though she had rewritten it seven times; and before her last illness she had made considerable progress on a second to be called "The Plantation." Part of the novel, according to Miss Mayfield's comment to me, was to be based on "my experiences running a family plantation at Beavers' Bend, Alabama. She feared the hold the land had on me—a matter we discussed frequently as one of the central themes of the novel."

The reaction of Sara's and Zelda's native state to Mencken's crusades against cultural aridity and race prejudice in the South was different from that of other southern states, such as Arkansas, where in both 1921 and 1931 editors, political associations, and state solons had urged legislation—even deportation—against the sage of Baltimore. When these measures failed of legal bases, the Arkansas state legislature stood for a moment of silent prayer for the misguided soul of H.L. Mencken. Alabama's ways were more subtle: she furnished him a wife, who succeeded in bringing him south on a visit in 1933. In Montgomery he was pleased to meet Grover C. Hall, editor of the *Advertiser,* who, according to Mencken's biographer, Edgar Kemler, had earlier presented him with an honorary membership in the Montgomery Kiwanis Club as well as a bona-fide copy of the Confederate States' Constitution "with the compliments and good wishes of the Cradle of the Confederacy from which he [was] snatching his bride." Sara's newspaper friend on the Dothan *Eagle,* Scottie McKenzie Frazier, rejoiced for the whole state when she reported that the woman who had once won the Alabama Federation of Women's Clubs' prize for free verse had now won "America's literary bachelor prize . . . . Sara Haardt was worth waiting fifty years for."

With these sentiments Mencken agreed; he found his five
years of marriage among the happiest of his life, just as he
had once been quite surprised that brains and charm could be
so united in a young instructor at Goucher College. It cannot
be argued that Sara greatly influenced Mencken's literary
work. He continued his philosophical and linguistic studies in
a new domestic environment that continually pleased him,
even to the extent of improving his table manners. It can be
argued, however, that Mencken influenced Sara Haardt's
perception of the Alabama she wrote about: an uncritical
view of southern sentimentality gave way to a new satirical
debunking and finally to a view of detached sympathy.
Despite his own needling, Mencken was himself at heart
something of a sentimental romantic about his German
ancestors and the days of his childhood in south Baltimore.
Certainly it can be said that Mencken guided an ambitious
Alabama girl in her literary career and that she achieved
steady improvement and sensitive insight into the craft of
writing during the eight years that she devoted full time to
literary work. The Alabama of fact and fiction are both in
her debt.

Of Sara's fellow townsman, Zelda Sayre Fitzgerald, the
summation is less obvious. Sheilah Graham in *Beloved Infidel*
quotes Fitzgerald as remarking to her about Zelda that they
would have been better off married to other people, that
they were harmful to each other. Whether such a statement
was only momentary judgment or considered hindsight is
difficult to know. And who can distinguish what is *harmful*
out of a lifetime of possibilities and chances? It can be argued
that the rejected "The Romantic Egotist" might never have
been rewritten into *This Side of Paradise* and that Scott
Fitzgerald might well have become a successful Broadway
lyricist or an advertising executive in Minnesota had not the
image of an Alabama girl goaded him into staking all on a
literary road to the instant fame and fortune that were
necessary to possess that image. Beyond doubt, together the

Fitzgeralds created in life and re-created on paper the archetypes of the Jazz Age, and Zelda always remained the controlling image for almost all of Fitzgerald's heroines. As a writer he profited from her practical criticism, and the literature of Alabama would be the poorer without Scott Fitzgerald's stories about the South. Moreover, Zelda Fitzgerald's fictional impressions of flaming youth, of Hollywood, of the Riviera and Paris, of Montgomery, and of the Fitzgeralds themselves would not exist without the driving, competitive spirit that Scott's own writing engendered in her. *Save Me the Waltz* is surely one of the most promising and genuinely appealing first novels ever produced by an Alabamian. If the Fitzgeralds destroyed each other, they did not more or less than countless others: "All men kill the thing they love." Together they created the most memorable literature of one phase of the tender, roaring Twenties.

A Bibliographical Note:

The sources for quoted statements and opinions are acknowledged, so far as possible, in the text itself. Among the numerous books on the Fitzgeralds and Mencken, the following were helpful: Charles Angoff, *H.L. Mencken: A Portrait from Memory* (1956); Carl Bode, *Mencken* (1969); Guy J. Forgue, editor, *Letters of H.L. Mencken* (1961); Edgar Kemler, *The Irreverent Mr. Mencken* (1950); William Manchester, *Disturber of the Peace: The Life of H.L. Mencken* (1951); Sara Mayfield, *The Constant Circle: H.L. Mencken and His Friends* (1968); Sara Haardt, *Southern Album*, edited with a preface by H.L. Mencken (1936); F. Scott Fitzgerald, *The Crack-Up*, edited by Edmund Wilson (1945); Sheilah Graham and Gerald Frank, *Beloved Infidel: the Education of a Woman* (1958); Sara Mayfield, *Exiles from Paradise* (1971); Arthur Mizener, *The Far Side of Paradise* (1951); Henry Dan Piper, *F. Scott Fitzgerald: A Critical Portrait* (1965); Andrew Turnbull, *Scott Fitzgerald*

(1962) and as editor, *Letters of F. Scott Fitzgerald* (1963); Nancy Milford, *Zelda* (1970). For first-hand information I am indebted to at least four persons. Miss Sara Mayfield answered questions about the relationship of these two women, and she was gracious enough to read an earlier version of this essay that appeared before her book on the Fitzgeralds. Zelda Fitzgerald's sister, Rosalind Sayre Smith, has been good enough to answer a query; and Elizabeth Tyler Coleman, a native of Montgomery and professor emerita of English at the University of Alabama, has been helpful. Andrew Turnbull before his death was generous about clearing up several points from his long study of the Fitzgeralds.

The essays, letters, short stories, and novels of Zelda Sayre Fitzgerald and Sara Haardt Mencken were of course the most significant sources for information about their literary careers.

8

The Prestons of Talladega and the Hubbards of Bowen: A Dramatic Note

THE three best-known plays about Alabama are Augustus Thomas's *Alabama* (1891) and Lillian Hellman's *The Little Foxes* (1939) and *Another Part of the Forest* (1946). Neither playwright is an Alabamian, but in their plays written half a century apart both demonstrate an interest in the historical, social, and political aspects of an Alabama they knew partially at firsthand.

Augustus Thomas (1857-1934) was born in St. Louis; his travels started at eleven when he went to be a page to the Missouri House of Representatives and later to the United States Congress. During his young manhood he served as transportation agent, railroad clerk, lawyer's secretary, box-office manager, amateur producer, dramatic and newspaper reporter, manager for Julia Marlowe, and agent for a mind reader. When he succeeded Dion Boucicault as adapter and reviser of plays for A.M. Palmer's Madison Square Theatre, his mature career began. *Alabama* was his first full-length play for Mr. Palmer, who after putting it into a week's rehearsal in 1891 delayed producing it until three imported British plays had failed. This was the first year of an international copyright protection for playwrights, and in a certain sense the year 1891 marks the end of the star-manager-adapter theater and the emergence of modern American drama.

The initial inspiration for the play occurred during the year 1884-85 when Thomas was touring the South with a theater company, he states in his autobiography, *The Print of My Remembrance.* The most penetrating cold and dampness he had ever known enveloped the "middle south," where the people had not yet recovered from the impoverishment of the Civil War. Many hotels, he writes, were poorly heated, and railway cars were often cold. At some junctions where the players waited they had "only a frame house with no fire in the stove."

On our way from Atlanta, which still bitterly remembered Sherman, we passed through Talladega to the busy little city of Birmingham. A story Mr. Owens [John E. Owens, a "fine, old actor" and theater owner in Charleston] had told us of a night in Talladega, the beauty of the town as we saw it, and especially the sight of a razed gateway to one old estate, impressed me. I laid there the scene of the first play I wrote some six years later for Mr. A.M. Palmer. Also, I named the play "Talladega," but Mr. Palmer throught that too exclusive for the theme, and we agreed on the title "Alabama."

Lillian Hellman, whose mother was Julia Newhouse from Demopolis, Alabama, was born in New Orleans in 1905 and spent the first six years of her life there under the benign supervision of the Negro servant Sophronia Mason, the probable model for Addie in *The Little Foxes.* After her father's shoe store on Canal Street failed when a partner absconded with the funds, the family went to New York, where her mother's Alabama family had already established themselves. But Miss Hellman returned regularly to the South, usually for six months of each year, until she was sixteen. After graduating from the New York public schools, she attended the new Washington Square branch of New York University despite her mother's preference for her own alma mater, Sophia Newcomb. Miss Hellman's emergence as a playwright was by way of the Hollywood scenario and as a play reader for Anne Nichols and for Herman Shumlin.

Both Thomas and Miss Hellman were interested in the dramatic possibilities of the decaying feudal society of Alabama after the Civil War as its people began rebuilding their plantations, stores, and towns. Thomas had known something of the tragedy of that war as the child of a father who had once managed a New Orleans theater for the entertainment of Federal troops, and as a young actor-writer he had traveled widely over the United States of the 1880's. According to Margaret Case Harriman's *New Yorker* Profile, Lillian Hellman became so fascinated by the Reconstructed South, to which she turned after the failure of her labor-management play, *Days to Come,* that she compiled monumental notebooks of two or three volumes, each four or five hundred typed single-spaced pages of data on contemporary history, local customs, factual anecdotes, political controversies, celebrities of the time, and long lists of likely names for characters. There is also clear evidence in the first chapter of her autobiography, *An Unfinished Woman,* that Miss Hellman used her mother's Alabama family, particularly her Uncle Jake, as models for the rapacious Hubbards. With the immediate success of *The Little Foxes* in 1939, starring Alabama's Tallulah Bankhead as Regina, Miss Hellman apparently felt that she had more than enough material for another play about the Hubbards and their imaginary little town of Bowden on a river not so far above Mobile. At any rate, in 1946 came *Another Part of the Forest,* a play about an earlier generation of Hubbards in the spring of 1880.

Across the state, Talladega in that same spring of 1880 was chosen by Augustus Thomas as the setting for his *Alabama.* The play was to deal with three generations of Prestons, who were as kind and understanding people as the three generations of Miss Hellman's Hubbards were for the most part evil and conniving. *Alabama* is now remembered as a sentimental social comedy with political overtones; Miss Hellman's plays

are regarded as tightly conceived experiments toward melodramatic tragedy.

Augustus Thomas's conversation about Talladega with
John Owens of Charleston, his glimpse of a ruined gateway,
and his impression of the town itself were more than names
and passing scenery. When he was ill in a room in The Lambs
club in New York some, five years later, he heard the actor
E.M. Holland playing the popular song "Down on the Farm"
on the piano. Induced by the music and his own fever, a
misty vision of the Talladega gateway appeared to Thomas:
"an old man walked through it, stood a moment, and was
joined by a young girl who took him by the arm and led him
obliquely out of the picture." This vision with its accompanying action was repeated two or three times during his
illness. After his recovery Thomas decided to write a play
about his dream of the Talladega gateway with the old man
and young girl; he would not try to "divine" their meaning
all at once—he "rather drifted with their story."

The resulting one-act play was praised by the Madison
Square stage manager, but he urged the young dramatist to
write a full-length one, emulating his success with *The
Burglar,* which grew in similar progression. When *Alabama*
was finished its central symbol was the ruined gateway of the
Preston plantation on the outskirts of Talladega, and the
climactic third act was a moonlit perspective of old Colonel
Preston with his granddaughter Carey guiding him through
the overhanging vines that covered the old brass cannon
behind one crumbling post.

The expanded play was partially tailor-made for certain
members of the company. The part for Holland was the
pompous Colonel Moberly, who had organized the Talladega
Light Artillery "for its salutary influence upon the blacks."
(Thomas had noticed these small militias in the Southern
towns he passed through in 1885.) The ingénue, Agnes Miller,
would play Carey Preston, and there would be the boy's role

of Lathrop Page for the juvenile, Harry Woodruff, as well as a comic Squire Tucker for the fat comedian Charles L. Wilson. The leading man—Captain Davenport, a Northern railroad builder, who is really Harry Preston in disguise—would be Maurice Barrymore, just as his son Lionel would later play the leading man in Thomas's last important play, *The Copperhead.*

Thomas observes all the conventions of the successful domestic comedies of the time with the love scenes for all ages played out to happy culminations. Old Colonel Moberly marries the widow Stockton; "Captain Davenport" wins his old sweetheart, cousin Mildred Page, whom he had been prevented from marrying by family objections before he courted Carey's long-dead mother; Lathrop Page is engaged to Atlanta Moberly, so named because she was born on the day that city fell to Sherman; and Mr. Armstrong, Captain Davenport's agent, finally wins permission to marry Carey Preston, "an Alabama blossom." The play also has its villain, Mr. Raymond Page. Being a man subject to bribes, a liar, and an ungallant fighter on the battlefield of Sharpsburg, he is easily routed by this righteous community.

Within the conventional framework of mistaken identity and happy, happy love, Thomas has contrived his major theme of one proud nation indivisible. Old Colonel Preston, disappointed that his West Pointer son Harry, unlike General Lee, chose to fight for the cause of the Union, at last comes to realize that the war is now over; and when he sees the sincerity of Carey's love for Mr. Armstrong, he knows he cannot prevent her from going through the ruined gates. "Captain Davenport," already recognized by the old servant Decatur and by Cousin Mildred, makes an appealing speech before he reveals himself to his father:

> I respect your feeling ... Colonel Preston, but I can't help thinking it is your personal view that blinds you. Things, sometimes, are too personal for a correct appreciation. The North

and South were two sections when they were a fortnight's journey apart by stages and canals. But now we may see the sunrise in Pennsylvania, and can take supper the same day in Talladega. It is one country. Alabama sends its cotton to Massachusetts—some of it grown very near your graveyard. The garment you have on was woven twenty miles from Boston. Every summer Georgia puts her watermelons on the New York docks. Pennsylvania builds furnaces in Birmingham. The North took some of your slaves away—yes—but one freight car is worth a hundred of them at transportation. Our resentment, Colonel Preston, is eighteen years behind the sentiment of the day.

At the end of the play Colonel Preston, the irreconcilable, has yielded ground, but his son Harry has also respected his father's wish that no Northern railroad cut through his plantation even if it means money for his swampy land. The railroad goes through, via the widow Stockton's. But the main family feud has been settled, because "hearts are a little bigger than sectional resentment."

Professor A.H. Quinn, who has surveyed the whole scene of American drama, finds an admirable directness of style in Thomas's *Alabama*—an absence of "fine writing" and a forward-looking use of the short sentence. However, a too frequent use of asides (like "My voice does not startle him— and the old eyes are grown dim with age"), too much triteness of diction, and too many uninteresting puns mar Thomas's style that was not to reach a level of stability until *Arizona* and *The Witching Hour*. *Alabama,* on the other hand, is entirely courageous in its subject matter: instead of dealing with times past in romantic lands Thomas undertakes a contemporary issue. Within the more rigid mold of the drama he sets out to achieve what the Alabamian Jeremiah Clemens attempted in his novel *Tobias Wilson: A Tale of the Great Rebellion* (1865), what De Forest succeeded in doing in his novel *Miss Ravenel's Conversion from Secession to Loyalty* (1867), and what Howells was hoping to accomplish in *A Hazard of New Fortunes,* published in the same year as

Alabama's first New York run. Like Howells Thomas looks upon the smiling aspects of life, but he looks with a degree of *veritism:* the Southern moonlight and magnolias are conspicuously present (in the moonlight Carey wears a magnolia at her throat), but so are the weeds and the poverty of poorly cultivated land; Negro voices across the bayou chanting "Carry Me Back" can be balanced against Colonel Moberly's boastful statement that he has been nominated for Congress by a strong group that "did not permit a bloomed niggah to the caucus." Compared with Belasco's *Madame Butterfly* (1900), Henry Arthur Jones's *Saints and Sinners* (1884), or Pinero's *Sweet Lavender* (1888), *Alabama,* despite its contrived plot and conventional stage devices, is a memorable achievement for a young man of thirty-two attempting to make his financial way in the commercial theater of the day. Professor W. Stanley Hoole, in tracing the contemporary reviews of the play (*Alabama Review,* April, 1966), has concluded that its reception in all sections of the country was indeed favorable both as drama and as propaganda. Even the Mobile *Register* (October 20, 1891) was complimentary after explaining that the actors' "drawl is not characteristic of Southern people any where . . . they [simply] raise and lower their voice more than do people of the North." The Talladega *Reporter* in the same month conceded the power of the play but objected to Talladega's being depicted as "an isolated community" when in reality it was now a city of 6000 people with railroads, furnaces, factories, water and gas works, and ten schools. That Thomas succeeded—at least for his generation—is best attested by the long run and many revivals of *Alabama* as well as by the remark of Colonel Henry Watterson of the *Courier-Journal* when the touring company reached Louisville: "This boy has done in one night in the theatre what I endeavored to do in twenty years of editorial writing."

Lillian Hellman's *The Little Foxes* (1939) and *Another Part of the Forest* (1946) provide two views of the Hubbards, the action of the sequel being twenty years earlier. The setting for *The Little Foxes* is "a small town in the deep South, the spring of 1900"; in *Another Part of the Forest* the designation is more specific, "June, 1880, the Alabama town of Bowden." Since "Hubbards Sons, Merchandise" and other surrounding landmarks remain fixed, the more exact setting of Bowden in "Rose County" serves for both plays, which make references to Mobile as the nearest urban center, approached by boat in 1880, by railroad or carriage in 1900. Miss Hellman explained to Lucius Beebe of the New York *Herald Tribune* that she did not originally plan two plays; but

> . . . you can imagine that after living with 'The Little Foxes' for several years I got to be on pretty chatty terms with the Hubbard Family . . . whom I cherish as one would cherish a nest of particularly vicious diamond-back rattlesnakes, but it did make me feel that it was worthwhile to look into their family background and find out what it was that made them the nasty people they were.

What emerges in *Another Part of the Forest* about the backgrounds of Ben, Oscar, and Regina is that their father Marcus, who came from the poverty of "carrying water for two bits a week," profiteered in the Civil War by running the blockade, dealing in salt for which he charged outrageous prices, and betraying the location of a Confederate training camp hidden in the swamp near Bowden, where twenty-seven trainees lost their lives. For these heinous deeds Marcus escaped lynching only by bribing a Confederate officer for passes proving false whereabouts. At the end of the war Marcus bought a large house with columned porticos, continued to see that Ben and Oscar ran the store, and acquired surrounding plantations. His wife Lavinia, knowing his wickedness, had become a mental case haunted by a sense of sin and consumed with a desire to build a school to educate Negroes, who are her only friends. In a community that holds his family as pariahs, Marcus turns to reading Greek and hiring musicians to come up from Mobile to play his amateur compositions and to allow him to participate in the ensemble. At twenty Regina is known to sleep with John Bagtry of Lionnet plantation and to have a half-incestuous relationship with her father; Oscar indulges in petty thievery and keeps company with prostitutes, while Ben calculatedly worms enough evidence from his mother to blackmail his father into turning over to him the family fortunes so that he can look to larger fields of operation. Ben buys into the Birmingham coal fields and forces Oscar to marry Birdie Bagtry after her cousin John runs off to Brazilian wars. Ben also forces Regina to marry Horace Giddens, a Mobile banker who has not yet become aware of her reputation. The family is thus ready to become little foxes, to spoil vines and tender grapes.

In *Another Part of the Forest* the old trickster Marcus is out-tricked by his eldest son Ben. In *The Little Foxes* Ben is out-tricked by Regina, who comments to him, "You'll be sort of working for me now." This interesting situation has been brought about by Oscar and his son Leo when they "borrow" Horace's railroad bonds to consummate the deal with Marshall and Company of Chicago, who will build a cotton mill in Bowden. Regina by refusing to administer Horace's medicine during one of his heart attacks in effect murders him so that she can control the bonds and thereby seventy-five per cent of the new Hubbard enterprise. She can now go to Chicago as she planned in *Another Part of the Forest,* and unlike Squire Tucker in *Alabama,* who cannot dream of exchanging Talladega's idyllic peace for Chicago's bustle, Regina tells Mr. Marshall, "Chicago may be the noisiest, dirtiest city in the world but I should still prefer it to the sound of our horses and the smell of our azaleas." But Ben, who whiffs from her daughter Alexandra the scent of Regina's guilt, remarks to his niece, "Alexandra, you're turning out to be a right interesting girl."

And the stage is set for a third drama about the Hubbard's trickery in the twentieth century. The family that sprang from a grandmother and a grandfather who were first cousins Oscar wishes, at the end of *The Little Foxes,* to preserve with a marriage between first cousins Leo and Alexandra. But perhaps Miss Hellman has decided that enough villainy is enough. She confessed in a recorded conversation with Richard G. Stern *(Contact 3)* that when she had finished *The Little Foxes* she was surprised to find that Regina "wasn't very nice . . . I think Regina was kind of funny; I was amused by her . . . I think most villains are funny. I felt deeply only about the girl [Alexandra]: I felt very strongly that she should leave the Hubbards." Pitted against Ben and Regina, however, and aided only by the faithful maid Addie and the pathetic alcoholic Aunt Birdie, Alexandra does not have an even chance to escape this nest of rattlesnakes.

The similarity between the Hubbards of Bowden and the Vaidens of Florence in Stribling's *The Store,* with its action set in 1885, is striking: both families' store is the key to their acquisition of decaying plantations of the aristocracy, both families' fortune is founded on theft and profiteering, both families seek through marriage social respectability and acceptance, and over both families hangs the shadow of lynchings and night riders and Klansmen. Just as Miltiades Vaiden seeks to marry Drusilla Lacefield Crowninshield, and being refused marries her daughter Sydna to acquire the appurtenances of aristocracy, so does Ben Hubbard say to Mr. Marshall, "But we are not aristocrats . . . [we] were in trade . . . . Twenty years ago we took over their land, their cotton, and their daughter." In the final analysis, both Miss Hellman's plays about the Hubbards and Stribling's three novels about the Vaidens are, for critical comfort, too close to sheer melodrama because characters, events, and resulting emotions are in excess of believable or warrantable facts. Miss Hellman dislikes the idea that she writes melodrama. If plays do "not convince you, or partly convince you," she writes in an introduction, they cannot be labeled "well-made" melodramas, if melodrama means "a violent dramatic piece, with a happy ending." As a dramatist, then, Miss Hellman poses her reader or viewer a neat puzzle: so expert and taut are her characterizations and dialogues that the plays are convincing so long as one is reading or listening to them, but a moment's reflection challenges the validity of horror piled on horror in the tradition of the late Elizabethan dramatists, like Webster and Ford.

By avoiding the "happy ending" Miss Hellman may save her plays from an indiscriminate labeling of melodrama, but despite the concern of her main characters with basic moral issues, the outcome is not quite the tragedy that offers resolution to emotional tension, nor is the ending inevitable in a Sophoclean sense. In *Another Part of the Forest* Marcus, having read the Greek tragedians and longed for noble sons, laments the wicked offspring fate has given him; but he deserves no better: his downfall is the downfall of an ignoble man. In *The Little Foxes* the servant Addie makes one of its most powerful speeches: "Well, there are people who eat the earth and eat all the people on it like in the Bible with locusts. Then there are people who stand around and watch them eat. Sometimes I think it ain't right to stand and watch them do it." That little foxes are allowed to go freely from one part of the forest to another is all mankind's responsibility, and the tragedy of Zan, about whom Miss Hellman feels "very strongly," is the tragedy of all gentle people who fall prey to the predatory and of all those who merely stand by or pass on the other side. All of us, then, must do more than watch on the Rhine; we must also watch on the Tombigbee to prevent the ruthless and the unthinking from victimizing the innocent. If we do not, we will have on our consciences the deaths of more than salesmen, like Willy Loman, whom the unthinking, brutal, mechanized world has broken and cast off. If Miss Hellman's rage for order drives her toward a new ethical rationale for modern drama, she should not weaken it by putting important speeches in the mouth of a house maid, where they seem too casual in a too glamorous garden of evil.

Miss Hellman also dislikes the fact that some critics insist that she writes "theme plays." Professor J.W. Krutch, for example, believes that these two plays consititute a "Marxian study of the decline of the Southern feudal aristocracy and the rise of the capitalistic exploiter." That aristocrats are dim-witted scoundrels more likeable than their victims "is according to formula." Because Miss Hellman thinks of her characters as pursuing their own destinies, she is "amazed" when others find much in *The Little Foxes* that she "hadn't intended—aristocracy against the middle class and so on." Having compiled "volumes" of typewritten background material, she should realize that since her characters do not live in a vacuum, her "implied" themes and suggested history may well represent more various views than she had intended. Even Ben believes, "There are hundreds of Hubbards sitting in rooms like this throughout the country. All their names aren't Hubbards, but they are all Hubbards and they will own this country some day." The Snopses, the Vaidens, and the Hubbards have been on the march.

In the half century that stands between Thomas's play about the Prestons and Miss Hellman's two about the Hubbards, the American theater came of age. Thomas in 1890 was a playwright in the literal sense of that term: he made his play to fit the theater company's personnel, and forthrightly based it upon the idea that a nation cannot afford to nurture sectional hate and prejudice. He put the strongest statement of this theme in the mouth of his hero at the very climax of the play. Furthermore, his scripts were prepared for acting, not for reading, his stage directions read "Squire entering 1 L: Moberly 3 L," and when Squire Tucker decides to "throw some pebbles at the window," the text reads merely "Business." In the 1880's and 1890's scripts were working guides for acting, not for pleasant reading. Within these conventions the playwright strove to be as skilled as he could, remembering that many of the same conventions plagued Shakespeare. Thomas revised only six of his later plays and provided them with informative prefaces to assist his later readers.

By the time Lillian Hellman writes, the conventions have somewhat changed. A play is prepared for reading as well as for acting. Eugene O'Neill believed that stage directions should be as expertly written as dialogue so that plays would read as pleasantly as novels. In this same vein Miss Hellman writes of Horace: "Then, suddenly as if he understood, he raises his voice. It is a panic-stricken whisper, too small to be heard outside the room." The present-day playwright must also be more subtle, eschewing the convenient "aside"—or at least reworking the device into some unusual pattern—for he will be judged not only in comparison with other dramatists but also with novelists. He cannot be as blatantly "thematic" as was once acceptable; like the novelist he must *show* rather than let his characters *orate.* Yet the spoken theatre has much the same limitations that it had hundreds of years ago. "It is a tight, unbending, unfluid, meager form in which to write." says Miss Hellman. "And for these reasons, compared to the novel, it is a second-rate form. (I speak of the form, not the content.)"

Thus the contemporary dramatist runs the risk of being adversely criticized from two directions: that of overstating intentions and that of having no thematic intentions. Miss Hellman has met both of these judgments. When Krutch spells out his social interpretations of the Alabama plays, he is forced to admit that none of "this" is spelled out by the playwright; on the other hand, Stark Young feels that "all the raging violence and blast and lurid vehemence does not proceed sufficiently from within the characters." A dramatist like Lillian Hellman, who feels strongly about her world of good and evil, and has already pointed to the play's central idea in its title about "foxes" or about another part of the ironically placid forest of *As You Like It,* can only reply: "I am a writer . . . I want to be quite sure that I can continue to be a writer and that if I want to say that greed is bad or persecution is worse, I can do so without being branded by . . . malice."

The only character in Thomas's play who would be at home with Miss Hellman's Hubbards is Raymond Page, a minor liar and petty thief by any Hubbard standards. But the two dramatists' concepts of moral forces have not prevented them from creating memorable social images of Alabama on the threshold of a new century. The railroad finally comes to Talladega; the cotton mill comes to Bowden by way of the internecine chicanery of the Hubbards. But the aristocratic Bagtrys in poverty and alcoholism scorn "the little foxes" to the end because "they kept a store"; Birdie marries Oscar but she despises him and hates her own son Leo. The aristocratic Colonel Preston may insist that the old cannon remain at the ruined gate, but a meadow lark now nests in its muzzle. The generous, forgiving Prestons will continue resistance, however seemingly ineffectual, toward people like the rapacious, unforgiving Hubbards: good and evil, two views of Alabama and of the world, the symbolic store and symbolic mockingbird will go on in endless opposition.

9

Philip Henry Gosse on the Old Southwest Frontier

THOUGH he remained only eight months in the new state of Alabama, the land and its people had considerable influence on the life of Philip Henry Gosse (1810-1888), eminent English naturalist and father of Edmund Gosse (1849-1928), poet, novelist, critic, and biographer of Victorian England. Philip Gosse's letters (*Letters from Alabama, U.S., chiefly relating to Natural History,* 1859) and Edmund's studies of his father (*The Life of Philip Henry Gosse, F.R.S., by his son Edmund Gosse,* 1890, and *Father and Son: A Study of Two Temperaments,* 1907) provide a vivid, intelligent appraisal of the Old Southwest in 1838. Indeed his eight months in Alabama, projected against the subsequent events of his life, can truthfully be called Philip Gosse's year of decision.

In the spring of 1838 the twenty-eight-year-old Gosse, whose "eye [was] toward Georgia or South Carolina," where he understood that "persons of education [were] in demand . . . both in mercantile and academic situations," sat at a candlelit table in the great hall of the museum of the Academy of Natural Science in Philadelphia. The young Englishman was the guest of the "venerable" botanist, Professor Thomas Nuttall: and he had already spent eight years working for the mercantile firm of Messrs. Harrison, Slade, and Company of Poole in Dorsetshire, where Philip had grown to manhood. These years had been spent, however, not in Poole, but in the company's frontier outpost of Cabonear, Newfoundland. He had also spent three years in Lower Canada farming, teaching school, and wielding "his butterfly net in the forests of Arcadia." Philip Gosse had probably learned as much as any living man about the entomology of Newfoundland and Canada.

Another Philadelphia *savant,* Timothy A. Conrad, the conchologist, suggested "that he would find a useful field for his energy in the state of Alabama; and . . . was so kind as to give him an introduction to a friend of his at Claiborne." After a stay of three weeks in the "Quaker city" the almost penniless Gosse found transportation as the only passenger on the dirty little schooner *White Oak,* bound for the port of Mobile. After a month's uncomfortable voyage via the West Indies, Gosse arrived on May 14 at the entrance of Mobile Bay, "a long, low tongue of land, with a lighthouse at the end of it."

Gosse lingered in Mobile only long enough to admire the plants and trees—the fan palms, honey locusts, and yuccas. He especially admired the "universality of open verandahs beneath which the inhabitants were sitting to enjoy the cool breath of evening," but he lamented the "exhalations" from the unhealthy mud flats where "dead horses and cows [were] suffered to be exposed on the shore, scarce out of the town." He took passage for Claiborne on a steamer up the Alabama, a river so winding that a "run of fifty miles [would] be then within three miles of where we were at first." On board he met Judge Reuben Saffold, who had recently retired from the State Supreme Court to devote more time to his Dallas County plantation near Pleasant Hill. Aided by his letter from Mr. Conrad of Philadelphia, Gosse was forthwith engaged to run a school for the Saffold children and those of neighboring planters. He promptly disembarked at King's Landing an hour before dawn and spent the rest of the day in a wagon at the pace of one mile an hour through "the romantic forest" to reach the Saffolds' house, "large, but rudely built .... The wide passage, with rooms on either side, which ran through the house, was completely embowered with lovely Southern creepers."

In a log cabin school with desks of "unsawn pine boards" Gosse instructed about a dozen children—"young ideas," he called them—who could "handle the long rifle with much more ease and dexterity than the goose-quill, and are incomparably more at home in 'twisting' a rabbit or treeing a 'possum, than in conjugating a verb." From May until Christmas, 1838, Gosse taught his school, painstakingly observed the plant and animal life, and looked with a shy, sharp eye on the social customs of the region. Underneath its uneventful surface, however, 1838 was his year of decision: what should Philip Henry Gosse do with his life?

His eight years in the lonely trading posts of Carbonear and St. Mary's in Newfoundland had at first been novel and then boring. Heretofore he had scarcely been in a position to make choices for himself: Philip had promised his Puritanical mother that at seventeen he would earn his keep as his brother William had done before him, and his relationship with Messrs. Harrison, Slade had been that of a six-year indentured engagement. Isolated as they were, these years had been a sort of practical schooling. He had devoured Adams' *Essays on the Microscope* and assembled a large insect collection of his own that followed him to Mobile and back to England. He had taught himself double-entry bookkeeping, and read all the novels he could get his hands on—even the heading of his diary entry for September 10, 1832, was labeled "the day before Sir Walter Scott died." In this same year he had come under the influence of the Wesleyan movement through his friends the Jaques and the Reverend Richard Knight. And in 1835 he had come under the influence of another trend of the time, an "unconscious Fourierism," as his son calls it. With Mr. and Mrs. Jaques, who were unsuccessful merchants in Carbonear, he had made his first choice; he decided on communal farming as the ideal life. "We could entomologize together in the noble forest, and, in peaceful and happy pursuits of agriculture, forget the toils and anxieties of commerce." But frosts came early to the sixty Canadian acres, and school "keeping" was neither pleasant not profitable when he earned only ten pounds for twelve weeks' winter teaching. So in the spring of 1838 Jaques drove him in a wagon across the border into Vermont, whence Gosse made his way by rail and boat to New York, Philadelphia, and Mobile.

In the mild Alabama climate, lodging in the home of a Mr. Buddy Bohanon near the Pleasant Hill school, and fortified with Judge Saffold's "liberal remuneration," Gosse could now sort himself out, as the English say. In his twenty-eighth year this young man of talents realized that he needed to choose his path from the many open to him, and during his Alabama sojourn he seems to have tried them out one by one.

Influenced by the Puritan upbringing of his mother and his more recent acquaintance with the Wesleyan movement in Canada, Gosse began to think seriously of Methodist mission work. In the Pleasant Hill church he delivered several sermons, and finally in December after the lively Quarterly Meeting at Brother Noseworthy's Selma chapel, Gosse decided "from the representations of Brother Hearne (the presiding Elder of this district) and Brother Noseworthy, and their persuasion, I have given up the thought of going to England, believing it my duty to labour here." Gosse re-turned to Pleasant Hill convinced that he "had a call to be a Wesleyan minister in Alabama . . . to spend his life there preaching and visiting." The full reasons for his not pursuing this path are never fully stated either in his own letters or in his son's account. A part of the explanation was probably what Philip Gosse calls "too much of a narrow bigotry" among Alabama Wesleyans. Even though he continued a serious interest in Methodism after returning to England, he discovered unhappily that "the rough discourses which had served in Alabama were not to the taste of the Methodists of Liverpool . . . [where] to studied refinement of the discourses, so thoroughly out of keeping with my own fresh and ardent feelings, distress me. I mourn over the degeneracy of Methodism." When Gosse left Alabama at Christmas, he had unconsciously decided that the life of a minister was not for him, but in England it took his conscious reasoning several more years to discover that the role of lay preacher among a sect known as the Plymouth Brethren and that of a writer of tracts like *Sacred Streams* (1850) for the Society for the Promotion of Christian Knowledge were his real religious milieus. In Alabama his spiritual crisis had come and passed: he had been swept up in the last phase of the Great Awakening that had followed the Carolina and Georgia immigrants into the Alabama frontier of the newly opened Indian lands during the 1830's. His son Edmund constantly refers to his father's "fresh religious zeal which he had roused in himself during his latest weeks in Alabama." This lingering Dallas County zeal was to color all his own life and indirectly that of his son, despite the dangerous "bigotry" that Philip Gosse had already perceived as a part of the evangelical persuasion.

His two avowed purposes in coming South were to seek a mercantile or an academic "situation." Since there was little hope of a mercantile success in a planter-dominated society, Gosse took advantage of Judge Saffold's offer to "keep" a school. He had been educated at a good preparatory school in Blandford, where he had learned Latin and the rudiments of Greek, but Gosse had largely taught himself what he knew of science, literature, and history. His first experience with teaching in a crude Canadian school had whetted his curiosity about the profession. In Alabama his school was equally crude, but he was decently paid and he had a wide latitude in what and how he taught. Reading between the lines of his own letters and his son's account, one can but conclude that the young Englishman was progressive and practical in his methods. He encouraged his pupils to go on collecting expeditions, gathering samples of insects and plants. He describes in detail how one of his students led him to the nest of a gold-winged woodpecker "in the decaying trunk of a pine-tree in Mr. Bohanon's peach-orchard." No doubt his pupils learned more from these nature "projects" than they did from their rudiments of Latin.

As the fall season wore on after the long summer, Gosse seemed to become depressed and probably malarial. At any rate, about the middle of November he writes: "My school has closed, another gentleman having been engaged to succeed me; in this . . . I see the hand of God." Gosse had discovered that teaching in a plantation community was scarcely a profession. He had been aware of the uncertainty in an academic situation, but he apparently believed that the choice of continuing a second year would be his. When he came to Dallas County, he had written to a friend:

> Schools here generally are not private enterprises, as in the old country, but the ordinary mode of procedure is as follows. Some half-dozen planters of influence meet and agree to have their children educated together, each stipulating the number of pupils to be sent, and the proportion of expense to be borne by himself. These form a board of trustees, who employ a master at a fixed salary, and . . . allow others to send children at a certain rate.

The individualistic and freedom-loving Gosse never again pursued the path of an educator except in a part-time capacity when he badly needed funds. In 1840, for example, at the Academy in Hackney, he taught geography while he was working on various manuscripts. And typically Gosse continued his own practical pedagogical experiments: he taught his pupils cartography by having them trace the pattern in the carpet, then a scaled plan of the school room to be followed by that of the building, the neighborhood, and the town itself.

Teaching and preaching were not the only paths that Philip Gosse tried in Alabama. He had learned the principles of drawing from his father, Thomas Gosse, a pleasure-loving itinerant miniature painter, who had been trained at the Royal Academy by Joshua Reynolds. In his lonely room at Mr. Bohanon's Gosse found time to perfect this skill. His son writes:

> There remains, as the principal memento of these months in the south still unpublished a quarto volume entitled *Entomologia Alabamensis,* containing two hundred and thirty-three figures of insects, exquisitely drawn and colored, the delightful amusement of his leisure hours in the schoolhouse and at home.

In addition to the pathway of illustrative art, Gosse was also toying with the idea of writing professionally about nature and life around him. He continued with enthusiasm his scientific journal until October, and he had long been in the habit of keeping a private diary. He had probably been planning a book based on his journals because as soon as he set sail from Mobile he began work on shipboard writing the first draft of what was to be called *The Canadian Naturalist* (1840), an account to be followed no doubt by a companion piece, "The Alabama Naturalist." The latter never came into being because Gosse had an opportunity in 1844 to investigate in greater depth the island of Jamaica, whose natural surroundings his friends at the British Museum assured him had never been scientifically studied. In Alabama Gosse gained his first experience in compiling careful notes on Southern birds, particularly the spectacular woodpeckers and the mockingbirds that he pronounced superior to nightingales—an experience that facilitated his *Birds of Jamaica.*

The chief evidence of his sincere interest in writing was the long letters to family and friends—often conceived as descriptive essays. A typical one begins:

Suppose you transport yourself (in imagination) to Alabama, and spend the day with me . . . . Well, then, here I receive you at old Buddy Bohanon's gate . . . . Walk in; we are just going to breakfast though it is but six o'clock. The "nigger wenches" have brought in grilled chicken and fried pork, the boiled rice and the homminy.—"Hold!" you say, "what is homminy?" Ah! I forgot you were a stranger . . . .

Another relates what must surely be one of the most lively accounts on record of a nocturnal 'possum hunt with lanterns, pine torches, slaves, horses, and dogs.

There are also little essays on such subjects as the sociology of the frontier village:

The Americans, in commencing a hamlet or village, always look forward to its becoming a city . . . . Nothing like attachment to a particular house, estate, or town exists in an American's breast; he always expects to sell his "improvements," and "move" to some other region; hence his residence has always a temporary character . . . . The accompanying sketch will give you an idea of the shops and groceries of Pleasant Hill, "our village."

Gosse apparently realized the value of his apprentice letters, for he published them serially in *The Home Friend,* and in 1859 he edited them as *Letters from Alabama.* By including his pen and ink sketches of scenes in Pleasant Hill and journeys up the Alabama River he provided a charming record of the Alabama he saw. Thus it was that Gosse began to discover the pathway of writing and drawing that would interest him all the rest of his life and provide most of his modest income. Alabama in 1838 had been his watershed: he had tried the rough and impractical courses of teaching and preaching, but he discovered genuine satisfaction in scientific writing and drawing.

Philip Gosse left Alabama not entirely because Judge Saffold and other "trustees" had chosen a new "master," but because of complicated, intertwined, and emotional reactions to his maturing self. He was obviously lonely, and his reserved, bookish bent did not help him make friends. He was without funds in a land of opportunity, for if he had had even a little capital he could have bought a few acres or set up a store—a new small version of the establishment of Messrs. Harrison and Slade that catered to the needs of the "planters"—in Newfoundland a term for the owners of schooners who "prosecuted one or both of the two fisheries of the colony, that for seals in spring and that for cod in winter."

More disturbing to the young Englishman were the crudity and lawlessness that were a part of these flush times on the frontier. Anti-British sentiment was strong in the Old Southwest. Many could recall the battles of Burnt Corn and New Orleans and the British conniving with Indians that sometimes led to massacres like the one at Fort Mims, the firing and cries of which Mrs. Saffold remembered hearing. Nothing could be sweeter to Alabama farmers than "the confident prophecy that Americans would shortly 'whip the British' " a third time.

A general attitude of lawlessness was illustrated memorably for Gosse by a neighboring plantation overseer who was offended by the proprietor of a traveling menagerie. The overseer and his friends retaliated by rolling the caravans of helpless animals down a steep ravine into a creek. There was also a duel fought in the neighborhood in which the combatants almost literally sliced each other to pieces with bowie-knives. And young Gosse would have been even more horrified if he could have read the letter C.C. Clay, Jr., sent his father, governor of the state from 1835-1837. In it young Clay describes lawless students at the University of Alabama who only four years earlier had terrorized the campus with their pistols, clubs, and brickbats aimed at the faculty and Dr. Alva Woods, the first president. Even after the students were expelled, they returned with cowhide whips to beat Dr. Woods.

Closely allied with this spirit of lawlessness was "our domestic institution" of slavery. Gosse was not a squeamish humanitarian; he had known about slavery before coming South. But he was not prepared to see Negro children "early inured, by kicks and cuffs, to bear the severe inflictions of the lash, &c., which await them in after life" or to hear "the shrieks of women under the cow-hide whip, cynically plied in the very courtyard beneath his windows at night." He was more troubled, however, by the reticence of his acquaintances to discuss the subject. Even among ministers and professors of the gospels he found "exactly the same jealousy of criticism and determination to applaud existing conditions, that could characterize the most dissolute and savage overseer, as he sat and flicked his boots with his cow-hide on the verandah of a rum-shop." According to his own son, Gosse wrote in his diary of 1838:

"What will be the end of American slavery? . . . . There are men here who dare not entertain the question. They tremble when they look at the future. It is like a huge deadly serpent, which is kept down by incessant vigilance, and by the strain of every nerve and muscle; while the dreadful feeling is ever present that some day or other, it will burst the weight that binds it, and take a fearful retribution."

For all of these reasons, then—social isolation, hopelessness of his financial status, repressed indignation at bigotry and narrowmindedness—Gosse bade the Saffolds farewell, packed his boxes and "cabinets," and, on board a river steamer heavily loaded with cotton bound for Mobile, ate his Christmas turkey. Much later in his life Gosse eschewed from his own household all such pagan and festive Christmas customs as turkey eating. When his servants surreptitiously gave his motherless eight-year-old son a piece of their Christmas pudding, the child burst into his father's study crying: "Oh! Papa, Papa, I have eaten of flesh offered to idols!" But in 1838 Gosse felt that at Christmas "There is something very romantic in sailing, or rather shooting, along between lofty precipices of rock, crowned with woods at the summit . . . bathed in golden light from the newly risen sun." At Mobile Gosse found in a warehouse his dilapidated "insect cabinet" from Canada, and, though in a "shocking condition," its contents were in reasonably good shape considering the jolting journey it must have had beginning with the frozen roads across the Vermont border in Mr. Jaques's wagon. On January 4, 1839, after spending some hours "walking through the public burial ground of Mobile," observing the "ridiculous" and "touching" epitaphs, Gosse says, "I went aboard the *Isaac Newton,* lying in the bay, and so bade adieu to American land, probably for ever." Ringing in his ears was the chant of Negro stevedores unloading cotton:

I think I hear the black cock say,
   Fire the ringo! fire away!
They shot so hard, I could not stay;
   Fire the ringo! fire away!
So I spread my wings, and flew away;
   Fire the ringo, etc.
I took my flight, and ran away;
   Fire, etc.
All the way to Canaday,
   Fire, etc.

If the wilderness of Alabama indirectly and somewhat accidentally helped Philip Gosse to see himself and his pathway to professional maturity, he also contributed significantly—beyond his years and time—to the historical record of what the Old Southwest frontier was like in 1838 as it began to fade into the settled environment of a Black Belt culture. Confined to Pleasant Hill as he was by his teaching, Gosse could travel but little. Yet his descriptions of his journeys from Mobile to King's Landing and back are memorable. About the only other journey he records is his horseback ride to Cahaba through the dense pine forests "with hardly a break save where the path dipped down, through a glade of thickly blossomed hydrangea, to some deep and treacherous 'creek' or rivulet." He crossed the Alabama on a flat ferry slowly pushed by "two old 'nigger fellows,'" to whom he paid a *"pic,"* one-sixteenth of a dollar, the smallest silver coin then current. Unfortunately located on low land at the confluence of the Cahaba and Alabama rivers, the once flourishing riverport had lost the capital in 1836 to Tuscaloosa, which was located on higher ground, free of flooding and fever epidemics. In June of 1838 Gosse found the little town of Cahaba in "general decay," a desolate collection of a few stores, a lawyer's office or so, and two or three business houses. Even the "groceries," as the rum shops were called, seemed "to spread the hospitality of their verandahs almost in vain."

Not only did Gosse record his impression of travel by horseback and river steamer along with the flora and fauna that caught his expert eye; he also noted such things as his neighbors' speech patterns. "Let me tell you," he writes to a friend, "one or two idioms, in which the Alabamians rejoice. To 'holler,' is used to express any sort of noise, as well as shouting . . . children remarked how the bee 'hollers in his hole.'" "To whip," he found to mean "overcome, as we use 'beat' . . . I reckon I can *whip* him at running." "To tote" was "to carry"; *"I toted the bucket,"* means "I carried the little tin pail in which the dinner was brought to school." "Branch" Gosse first understood to mean "a small tree" until he discovered it meant a "small river or creek." "Trousers" were "pantaloons"; and a "jacket" was a "roundabout." "Right" he found must frequently be equated to the "old English *very*"; "good" often meant "well." "Inquiry" he found most often pronounced *en-quiry,* and "idea" *idée.* Lest his English correspondent feel superior, Gosse reminds him: "Still I have never heard an American fall into the blunder of calling a white egg a 'wite hegg,' as thousands of your countrymen do." Good unschooled linguist that he was, Gosse summed up his observations in this way: " . . . the inhabitant of one district has no right to assume any superiority over one of another who uses a phrase differing from his own . . . knowledge of such differences may be a legitimate source of amusement, and possible instruction."

Not all of Gosse's record of Alabama is serious and sober. At the end of his long narration of the 'possum hunt in Dallas County, he remarks:

> The propriety of correct classification was impressed on me during my examination [of the 'possum]. I inadvertently spoke of it as "a singular creature;" but *creature,* or rather "critter," is much too honourable a term for such an animal, being appropriate to cattle. The overseer promptly corrected my mistake. "A 'possum, sir, is not a critter, but a varmint."

To a correspondent who apparently desired more narratives like that of the 'possum hunt Gosse replies that his observations are "slight and disjointed," that he has no story to tell—rather he thinks of his journals as "passages in the life of a spider . . . unpublished memoirs of a beetle . . . notes on the domestic economy of a fly."

This smiling British humor is markedly in contrast with the broad American guffaw of the frontier that also appealed to the more reserved Gosse. He relates, for example, the story of "a fellow from the North," who charged a considerable entrance fee for his lecture that was to reveal an infallible preventive for the thefts of squirrels. Though the fee was excessive, the farmers willingly paid it because squirrels were the worst of all the depredators of their cornfields. Gosse himself joined the assembly because he expected to hear something of interest to a naturalist. After a long account of squirrels and their methods of wasting fields, the speaker concluded:

"You wish," he said, "to hear my infallible preventive, the absolute success of which I am able to guarantee. Gentlemen, I have observed that the squirrels invariably begin their attacks *on the outside row* of corn in the field. *Omit the outside row,* and they won't know where to begin!"

With the money in his pocket the con man made a hasty exit and leaped into his saddle. After a "moment of stupefaction and roar of anger" the audience dissolved in "good-humoured laughter." This kind of yarn was typical of the tastes of the frontier, and it was shortly to become the hallmark of newspaper stories and later volumes of sketches like Johnson J. Hooper's *Some Adventures of Captain Simon Suggs* (1845) and Joseph G. Baldwin's *The Flush Times of Alabama and Mississippi* (1853).

As an accurate observer of the life about him in 1838 Gosse records that "very many of the houses, even of the wealthy and respectable planters, are built of rough and unhewn logs, and to an English taste are destitute of comfort to a surprising degree." Compensations, however, had always abounded, at least for Gosse, in "an inexpressive grandeur of these primeval forests" and in the delightful and bountiful food like cornbread "woffles," peaches of such "flavour that no wall can impart in a colder climate," and "deservedly esteemed" watermelons unknown in England. His final estimate of the people and the frontier region he had come to know is best summarized in his own words:

The manners of the Southerners differ a good deal from those of their more calculating compatriots, the Yankees . . . . In many respects the diversity is to the advantage of the former; there is a bold gallant bearing, a frank cordiality, and a generous, almost boundless hospitality, in the southern planter . . . . But the abiding thought that "the people," as being the source of law, are therefore above law . . . is much more frequently made operative in the South than in the North.

Though Gosse never returned to the United States after his departure in January, 1839, he did return to the New World from 1844 to 1846, when he visited Jamaica. This venture provided material for two of his best books, *The Birds of Jamaica* (1847) and *A Naturalist's Sojourn in Jamaica* (1851); the former remains a classic of its genre, and the latter, along with the work of Henry David Thoreau, began to establish something of a new trend in books about nature that Gosse rightly believed had been too much concerned with "a science of dead things, a necrology." So well did he succeed in drawing nature as something ever living and changing that he received the commendation of Charles Darwin.

When the scientific crisis of his century approached, however, Gosse was not prepared to embrace its thesis. Even though his monographs on zoophytes issued in 1855 and 1856 show him prepared to grasp the doctrine of biological evolution, Gosse's "belief in a direct creative act from without, peopling the world with a sudden full-blown efflorescence of fauna and flora, was a part of [his] very being, and he would have abandoned the entire study of science sooner than relinquish it." When, in the summer of 1857, Lyell, Hooker, and Darwin decided that the leading scientific writers needed to be briefed on the views Darwin and Wallace would expound before the Royal Society, both Darwin and Hooker talked to Gosse, trying to solicit his understanding and help. His reply, after much private thought was *Omphalos: An Attempt to Untie the Geological Knot,* published in November of that year. The work was a philosophical one that had as its purpose to reconcile what he foresaw as a coming split between Christians and their Bibles on the one hand and Lyell, Darwin, and like-minded scientists on the other. Taking the position that geological evidence was circumstantial at best, Gosse tried to show that because all "life is a circle . . . produced full grown by the arbitrary will of God, [it] would certainly present the

stigmata of a pre-existent existence." Or, "when the
catastrophic act of creation took place, the world presented,
instantly, the structural appearance of a planet on which life
had long existed." Scientists and Christians alike were
repelled by this concept. The kindly Charles Kingsley wrote
Gosse that he could not "give up the painful and slow conclusion of five and twenty years' study of geology, and
believe God has written on the rocks one enormous and
superfluous lie."

Though his son Edmund in both the *Life* and in *Father
and Son* points out that his father was not at his best in
1857, his wife having recently died and the family having
isolated themselves in a new house on the Devonshire coast,
one can but wonder what effect that year of decision in 1838
in Alabama unconsciously played in Philip Gosse's role in the
great drama of evolution. The fact that he did not remain as a
Methodist missionary in the Old Southwest seemed to haunt
him all through the 1840's and 1850's as he struggled to be
both lay preacher to the Plymouth Brethren and practicing
scientist at the same time. *Omphalos,* that strange work of
philosophical geology—Gosse being neither philosopher nor
geologist—may well have been his emotional attempt to pay
his debt to his personal creator whom he believed he had
partially betrayed in his youth. And in a kind of grand irony
some of the "narrow and bald" views he had resented in the
Alabama Methodists had now manifested themselves in him:
Nature was perhaps more cyclic than even Gosse suspected.
His son Edmund, too, shares in this unconscious irony:
protesting his father's fanaticism he began his career by aping
the Pre-Raphaelites and seeking things Swinburnian, only to
create his real masterpiece toward the end of his career by
writing an analysis of his father's Puritanism: *Father and Son,
A Study of Two Temperaments.*

However one may explain the strange character of the
motives that prompted Philip Gosse, like Louis Agassiz of
Harvard, to challenge his colleagues and gainsay the evidence

of his own research, one cannot deny that the memories and mementos of his Alabama past were both pervasive and subtle. One small but very tangible example of this attitude is Edmund's description of his father's favorite book, the 1798 Delphin edition of Virgil's *Eclogues* that had been his father's constant traveling companion. "On the sheepskin cover," Edmund writes affectionately in *Father and Son,* "there was a great scratch that a thorn had made in a forest of Alabama."

Index